Portraits

OF NATIVE AMERICANS

Portraits
OF NATIVE AMERICANS

IAN WEST

SMITHMARK

A Salamander Book

This edition published in 1995 by
SMITHMARK Publishers, a division of U.S. Media Holdings, Inc.,
16 East 32nd Street, New York, NY 10016.

1 2 3 4 5 6 7 8 9

SMITHMARK books are available for bulk purchase for sales promotion and premium use. For details write or call the manager of special sales, SMITHMARK Publishers, 16 East 32nd Street, New York, NY 10016; (212) 532-6600.

ISBN 0-8317-5516-4

Printed in Singapore

Credits

Project Editors: Christopher Westhorp and Richard Collins
Designer: Mark Holt
Picture Researcher: Rachel Boone
Filmset: SX Composing Ltd, England
Mono reproduction: Pixel Tech Ltd, Singapore

Page 1: A tattooed Inupiat-Inuit mother with her child.
Page 2: A highly evocative portrait of a Maricopa man from 1899 entitled 'A Nation's Cry.'
Pages 4-5: Navajo Indians on horseback near the base of Shiprock, New Mexico.
Page 7: Portraits from the nine cultural regions of North America. By row, from the left: Top - (Southeast) Seminole woman, (Southwest) Hopi mother and daughter), (Plains) Osage man Sho-she; Center - (Plateau and Basin) Flathead man Antoine Moise, (California) Nisenan boy, (Northwest) Kwakiutl man; Bottom - (Subarctic) Chipewyan-Cree girl, (Arctic) Inupiat-Inuit man, (Northeast) Potawatomi child.
Page 143: Pueblo girls from Acoma in traditional shawls.

Contents

DEC   1999

Introduction

These early photographers were frightening people - 'Shadow Catchers' - to many of their reluctant subjects, taking 'Spirit Pictures' which the uncomprehending Indians felt might result in them losing some part of themselves to the 'strange box of bad medicine.' However, once they realized that the instrument could do no harm to them most complied with reluctance.

The earliest known photograph of an American Indian is that of the Reverend Peter Jones, a halfbreed Mississauga, taken by Hill and Adamson in about 1844 when he was on a visit to England. It was not until the late 1800s that photographing these people became a popular and lucrative business. It may have been the popularity in the east of tales of the frontier and its Indians that increased the popularity of pictures of the 'Wild West' and its inhabitants. Up until this time the only visions of this country had been in the paintings of artists such as Catlin, Bodmer, Moran and Charles Bird King. People in the east were also beginning to see delegations of Indians in the big cities, particularly Washington, coming to discuss their problems with 'The Great White Father'.

It was toward the end of the nineteenth century that photographers took their equipment into the field to record many of the fast-disappearing ceremonies, dances and general way of life of the Indians. This was the period of the so called 'Vanishing Indian' and one of the best known photographers of this time was Edward S. Curtis. His laudable intention, which became his life's work and probably caused his death, was to record every phase of Indian life in every tribe in the United States. But his pictures were often posed and contrived and his subjects dressed in studio props so that, although the views and portraits are exceptional, they should be viewed with some scepticism. Some mystery surrounds another collection of portraits which were taken on behalf of Rodman Wanamaker, a rich department-store magnate, who also wished to record Indian life before it 'vanished.'

To this end he organized three expeditions for photographic purposes, one in 1908, one in 1909 and the last in 1913. It is not certain but these photographs could have been taken by J.K. Dixon who led all three expeditions and wrote a book containing portraits of most of the then prominent chiefs. The portraits in the book, taken on the first two expeditions, are fine if rather reminiscent of the 'Noble Savage'-type. But those taken on the 1913 expedition appear to have been doctored by extensive retouching and tricks of light and either give the impression of the stereotype 'noble savage'-image again or the other extreme, the 'bloodthirsty savage'.

Probably the 'truest' photographs are of the type that appear in this book and, devoid of romanticism, are what one could call 'ethnological portraits.' Many such pictures were taken by photographers accompanying exploring parties or scientific expeditions and surveys when the object was to gather all types of data and information of the area and its people.

At this time Studio photographers were also doing a good trade in Indian pictures but the great problem here was that many of them did not bother to label their work. Other photographers made copies of their rival's work and collectors of such material failed to keep records of provenance or, if known, who the person in the photograph actually was. Some of these studio portraits also need to be carefully studied for inaccuracies and the use of 'studio props.' Few of the Indian sitters had much left of their own native dress at that time but most of the studios had small collections of artifacts and clothing and because they did not know, or were not bothered, about tribal distinctions in clothing or accoutrements, they dressed their clients in an assortment of costumes just to make them look, in their eyes, more 'Indian.'

The other type of photographs taken were those wanted and used for scientific purposes where the Indian was pictured full-face and profile, and at the same time had facial measurements taken, rather like a criminal, for institutions such as The Bureau of American Ethnology. History does not record how the subjects viewed these arrangements but some were even persuaded to have plaster casts made of their faces. No matter how the pictures were taken it is hoped that those shown here will not only highlight the skill of these early photographers but will also show the poignancy of a people who did not vanish and, although conquered, were not defeated.

The Southeast

ALABAMA • APALACHEE • APALACHICOLA
ATAKAPA • BILOXI • CADDO • CALUSA
CATAWBA • CHEROKEE • CHICKASAW
CHITIMACHA • CHOCTAW • COUSHATTA
CREEK • HOUMA • KOASATI • MOBILE
NATCHEZ • SEMINOLE • TUNICA • YUCHI

Within the boundaries of the Mississippi River to the west, the Ohio to the north, and the great sweep around the northern part of the Gulf of Mexico taking in the Florida Peninsula and up the Atlantic coast to join with the northeastern woodlands area, was the home of the southeastern farmers.

In prehistoric times some of the most highly civilized tribes in America lived here. Through their connections with the great civilizations of Mexico they built huge temples and effigy mounds in the form of animals and birds, most of which, in spite of archaeological work, hold their secrets to this day.

Farming was practiced by the women after the men had cleared the fields and a large variety of crops were planted. When harvested there was much ceremony and ritual; the Green Corn Dance was prominent and marked the end of the year. Fishing was also an important part of their subsistence and large quantities of shellfish were gathered from the lakes and rivers. The forests and swamps were full of deer and other game so that hunting also played an important part in their lives.

With the arrival of the Spanish and then the French and English the tribes were plundered and demoralized with smallpox and other diseases and finally were forcibly removed to Indian Territory, now Oklahoma. Many, however, still survive today in small groups in their original homelands.

The picture gives a good example of the country in southern Florida, a semi-tropical area of forests, rivers, lakes and swamps. The lonely village in Big Cypress Swamp is a typical Seminole community of palm thatched houses called 'Chickees' - open-sided buildings ideally suited to the typically hot and humid climate.

Choctaw

Muskogean language family.

This man is wearing a 'long shirt' with patchwork bindings and a cape-type top. He has a characteristic beaded bandolier over his right shoulder and a long loop of alternately colored beads across his left shoulder, these match his multi-strand necklace.

He may be a ball player but he is certainly not dressed to play, such players would be stripped to breechclout only and bare feet.

The Choctaws, amongst all the Southeastern tribes, seem to have attached great importance to all games and it is said that as they did not have strong religious beliefs or ceremonies they were more active in social and recreational activities, which may account for their somewhat advanced condition when first encountered by whites. Certainly the ball game was an important event prepared for long in advance and preceded by a special dance as well as performances of magic by the medicine men trying to outdo each other for the benefit of their own side. Players' numbers varied but according to Catlin, who witnessed many games in 1834 during his visit to the Choctaw, six to eight hundred young men took part, many being seriously injured in the resulting mêlée.

The Choctaw were the largest of the Muskogean tribes and were a generally quiet and intelligent people who practiced an agricultural life style growing all manner of crops, the most important of which was corn. Some hunting and fishing was also done. They became deeply involved in the various wars amongst the French, British and finally the Americans before some of them were removed to Oklahoma, the remainder staying in their old territories in Mississippi and Louisiana. By this time they had adopted many of the white man's customs and were known as one of the so-called 'Five Civilized Tribes.'

Creek

Upper and Lower Creek. Muskogean language family.

Sports and games were extremely important to the Creeks and some were deeply embedded in their religion. The man in this 1860 photograph is holding a game stick in his left hand, which has the bent-netted hoop for catching the ball. There was much ritual attached to games and each player wore special clothing and accoutrements, although this man does not appear to be dressed to play. He wears a cloth shirt crossed over which are two fine beaded bandoliers and on his chest are three metal gorgets. His hat, a remnant of the old style turban, has a decorated metal crown and is surmounted with ostrich feathers obtained in trade.

There are several types of ball game of which the most frequently played was the single-pole game in which men and women of all ages competed against each other. The point of the game was to hit an object attached to a tall pole in the center of the field or even the pole itself above a certain mark. This game was always played in fun with a great deal of good humor and invariably the scorer, a man, was accused of cheating by the women, who usually won anyway. There was great skill in catching the small ball and in hitting the post and the game was considered to be good training for the bigger inter-town stickball game. This was a much more formal occasion and was played by men and boys only with long preliminaries and preparations for a week beforehand consisting of fasting and dancing. The night before the game the women performed a dance to strengthen their side's 'medicine' against their opponents. Each player wore a special costume for the game and was painted on the face and chest and, whilst this was being done, some men would ask a medicine man to scratch their arms and legs to improve muscle power and prevent stiffness. It was generally a rough game and, with tempers running high, casualties were frequent.

THE SOUTHEAST

Seminole

Muskogean language family.

The fine-looking gentleman in the photograph portrays the aristocratic looks of his Creek ancestry and proudly wears the costume of the area, which was probably outdated by 1900. His traditional belted tunic type loose shirt, known as a 'long shirt' and which was probably red with white spots, is crossed with a beautifully beaded bandolier bag on one side and a long hand-woven sash on the other. He has a decorative scarf around his head and a bandana knotted round his neck His cloth front-seam leggings are beaded round the ankles and have tabs which flare over the tops of his moccasins, and are further enhanced by loom-beaded garters tied below the knees with long fringes. Moccasins seem to have been mostly worn by men while women preferred to go barefoot, although Seminole one-piece moccasins are probably the easiest to make and the most comfortable to wear. Those worn by the man seen here are undecorated, which was usual, but sometimes a bead-decorated cloth panel was sewn over the front seam and to the heel on either side.

The Seminole people are descendants of the Upper Creek refugees pushed south by the Creek War of 1813-14. The name Seminole is derived from the Spanish word Cimarrón, meaning 'wild,' and refers to the fact that these people had moved into a wild,unoccupied territory. As the Muskogean language has no R sound the original Spanish sound Cimarrónes became Simalones and eventually Seminoles.

The constant colonial wars between the Spanish, British and Americans unavoidably involved nearly all the tribes of this area and following the first war of 1813-14 came the second, which is reputed to have been the most costly war ever fought by the US Army. No official treaty was ever signed by the Seminole and to this day they are supposedly still at war with the United States.

Old Tallahassee

Seminole

Muskogean language family.

The three Cow Creek Seminole ladies with the fixed stares are possibly mother and daughters and were photographed in this studio portrait in 1917. They are all wearing what is now regarded as typical Seminole clothing, but fashions in this area have changed over the years and in the distant past clothing was of skin. This was changed when they were able to obtain cloth - which was cooler - once they had settled in the semi-tropical climate of the Florida Everglades. By about 1880 women were wearing long full skirts with a flounce just above the knees, with simple decoration of appliqué designs. These skirts were made of calico or gingham with a belt at the waist, over which they wore short blouses with a cape leaving a bare midriff. Sewing machines came into use in about 1890 and women's capes became longer and longer until the sleeves disappeared altogether. The flounce was moved to the hips and bright solid-colored cloth became popular with lots of patchwork designs. Following this the flounce disappeared and the bands of patchwork are often of commercial rick-rack and capes are made from silk, rayon or nylon. These women show the patchwork dress at its peak, as it is now only worn at festivities and for the benefit of tourists and the tourist market. The wearing of multi-stranded necklaces has always been an almost obligatory part of a woman's dress outfit, and were originally made of shell and later trade beads. The girl on the left of the photograph has her hair done in the old style, wrapped around a hoop to create a curved bang across the forehead or to the side. The girl on the right has a straightforward rolled quiff, whilst the older lady appears to have given up altogether! She has, however, decorated the front of her cape dress with a row of silver coins.

The Southwest

APACHE • COCHIMI • COCOPA • HAVASUPAI
HOPI • HUALAPAI • KARANKAWA • MARICOPA
MOHAVE • NAKIPA • NAVAJO • OPATA • PAIPAI
PAME • PAPAGO • PERICU • PIMA • PUEBLO
(ACOMA • COCHITÍ • HANO • ISLETA • JÉMEZ
LAGUNA • NAMBE • PICURÍS • POJOAQUE • SAN
FELIPE • SAN ILDEFONSO • SAN JUAN • SANDÍA
SANTA ANA • SANTA CLARA • SANTO DOMINGO
TAOS • TESUQUE • ZIA) • SERI • TARAHUMARA
TONKAWA • WALAPAI • YAQUI • YAVAPAI
YUMA • ZUNI

*T*he greatest part of the Southwestern desert area lies in Arizona and New Mexico with the edges running into small parts of Colorado and Texas and the northern parts of Mexico. Culturally speaking it can be divided into four main divisions: the Pueblos, the Navajo, the Apache and the desert farmers.

The history of the Pueblo people goes back many thousands of years but they became famous in historic times for their fine textile weavings, decorated pottery, and the wealth of their colorful ceremonies, costumes and dances, many of which were to bring fertility to the people and soil.

The desert farmers such as the Pima and Yuma were generally peaceful peoples who were friendly towards the white invaders who helped subdue their Apache enemies, who, although few in number, were formidable warriors and were the cause of an extended war with the United States before they were finally overcome.

The warlike Navajo were also subjugated militarily and became successful sheep and goat herders famous for their beautiful woven rugs and blankets and their jewelry. Their reservation is the largest in the United States today.

The photograph shows what is almost certainly the old Hopi town of Oraibi situated on the Third Mesa and said to be the oldest still inhabited town in the United States. Hopi men can be seen emerging from the underground kiva, a male lounging place as well as the site where religious and secret ceremonies took place.

Apache

Eastern and Western Apache. Athabaskan language family.

This fine photograph shows an Apache who was, for some obscure reason, named after the then President of the United States, James A. Garfield. By the 1850s photographers were producing pictures from glass plate negatives and because this method was time consuming and laborious it was only used by professionals. Over the years these fragile plates often crack, such marks appearing on the printed photograph, and the line running across this man's face shows such a crack.

He is dressed in Plains-style costume, typical of the Western Apache who had a close association with the southern Plains tribes. His hair is parted in the center and his braids are wrapped with otter skins. He wears a dentalium shell choker with a conch shell center disc. Over the white man's white shirt and waistcoat, or vest, he wears an otter-skin bandolier inset with trade mirrors. He has painted white stripes from his lower eyelids in a curve to his chin, the meaning of which would be known only to him, although similar white circles often represented tears shed for comrades lost in battle.

Noted for their warlike disposition the Apache raided both white and Indian settlements as far south as Mexico, for whose people they seem to have had a particular hatred. Such leaders as Cochise and Victorio kept up a constant war along the frontier, much of the trouble being attributed to mismanagement by the agents and other civil authorities. Geronimo was another great war leader and it was his capture and deportation to Florida that finally brought peace to this part of the country.

Apache

Eastern and Western Apache. Athabaskan language family.

Of the various tribes making up the Apache nation, one of the largest groupings was that of the Western Apache, itself composed of a group of sub-tribes called the Apache Peaks, Arivaipa, Cibeque, Fort Apache, Mazatzal, Pinal, San Carlos, Tonto and White Mountain Apaches, collectively also known as Coyoteros from the Spanish for 'wolf men' - probably because of their nomadic existence.

Known as 'The Scourge of the Southwest' the Apache had a well-deserved reputation as fierce warriors and their arrival from the north had an impact on the southwest second only to that of the coming of Europeans. Their raiding throughout the area and into Mexico became legendary. In historic times US Army troops under the commands of Generals Crook and Miles campaigned against them for years until the surrender of the great chief Geronimo in 1886 brought an end to the fighting. The photograph, by A. Frank Randall, shows two White Mountain Apache hunters from San Carlos Reservation in 1888 in typical Apache dress comprising a cloth skirt or apron and cloth headband and high-top skin boots, ideal for protecting the feet from cactus spines. The young man on the left appears to be wearing US Army-issue knitted socks! Their weapons consist of long hunting bows and arrows in contrast to the shorter variety used by the horse-riding Plains Indians. The Apache also used horses and there is a story told that a man could ride a horse almost to death and give it to an Indian who would get many more days riding out of it and then, when stolen by an Apache, it was eaten! Today these Apache have become successful as stockmen and live on the San Carlos and Fort Apache reservations in Arizona.

Hopi

Uto-Aztecan language family

*T*he Hopi or Peaceful People were also sometimes known as Moqui or Moki by their neighbors. They occupied three of the western pueblos near the eastern boundary of northern Arizona and right in the center of the great Navajo Reservation. They were a peaceful people, as their name for themselves implies, but the Spanish explorers had found them as early as 1540 and missions were set up in the 1620s when the people became slaves and their culture nearly crushed, ensuring their involvement in the Pueblo Revolt when the missionaries were killed and the churches burnt. They now lead a mostly pastoral existence tending herds of sheep and goats and gardening on the bottom lands below the high mesas where they grow maize, peaches, pumpkins, beans, squash, melons and chilies, and are well known for their fine weavings and basketry.

The young maiden in the photograph taken by Carl N. Werntz is Da-wa-uni-ci from Mishongnovi. She has her hair done in the typical side-whorl style of post-pubescent girls and she wears bead and silver jewelry.

Mohave

Yuman language family.

Being photographed was a traumatic experience for many Indian people, who believed that the resultant picture took away their spirit. These two are more sophisticated but still appear rather apprehensive in this studio portrait taken at Needles, California, in 1884 by J.C. Burge.

The picture is sometimes wrongly labelled Pima and attributed to Ben Wittick, who formed a brief partnership with Burge in 1886 and some confusion occurs in the labeling of some of the studio portraits.

This young couple are wearing white man's clothes with some native additions - the boots of the man appearing rather incongruous, especially beside his wife's bare feet. The cloth skirt, waist band and trimmed cape became a distinct style for Mohave women and the beaded collar a very popular item amongst them and their neighbors. This very distinctive form of decoration was a symbol of wealth and fashion and, although few old examples survive because of their mortuary custom of burning the property of the deceased, it is still made and worn today as part of traditional costume.

The Mohave were a warlike tribe living a desert existence along the Colorado River. They practiced little hunting, preferring to grow fruits and vegetables such as beans, squash, melons, pumpkins and various nuts, as well as catching some fish. Their principal crop was maize, the ground prepared and planted by the men but women helped in the harvesting, husking and drying of the crop. Today the Mohave survive by farming, leasing land and wage-earning in the local towns; little of their former culture survives.

Navajo

Athabaskan language family

Known to themselves as Dine or Dene - The People - the Navajo occupy the largest reservation in the United States of America included within which is the reservation of the Hopi.

From earliest times the Navajo harassed the pueblos and the first white settlers, and from 1849, after the United States had taken possession of New Mexico, campaigns were launched against these warlike people from the north. But it was not until 1863 when Colonel Kit Carson turned the tables on them and invaded their territory, devastating their fields and crops, that their power was finally broken.

This photograph from 1923, entitled 'The Silversmith's Daughter,' shows an obviously apprehensive young girl wearing a traditional Navajo woman's outfit of the period consisting of a flared white cotton skirt surmounted by a red velvet blouse. Her wrists are encircled with cast silver bracelets and she wears several necklaces, including one of turquoise and another with loops of trade beads ending in what is known as a Naja, a word meaning crescent. The double semicircle of silver was probably brought to the Southwest by the early Spanish explorers as part of their horse decorations. The crescent is of antique origin and came to the Spanish via the Moors. As a single piece it was a popular bridle ornament copied and doubled by Navajo silversmiths to become a necklace embellishment. Also suspended from these necklaces are pieces of abalone shell, no doubt obtained in trade.

Navajo

Athabaskan language family

*T*his photograph by Pennington, shows a woman wearing a native-style blanket and carrying her baby in a cradle board on her back.

The birth of a child was a special blessing and the occasion for much celebration; children holding a very high place of honor in most tribes. Cradle boards were an important part of the baby's equipment and decoration varied according to tribe. Amongst the Pawnee, particularly, the designs and carvings on the board's backing had much symbolic meaning. Arapaho women made a distinctive type of quilled cradle which involved much symbolism and ceremonial construction. Men seem to have made most of the board cradles and the Navajo's were constructed using two pieces of wood lashed together and a wooden foot rest. Over the front of the cradle was fixed a bent wooden hood, which protected the infant who was wrapped and held in place with soft buckskin ties: the one in the photograph is of this type. They also made cradles of basketry, and the so-called 'hurdle'-type which was constructed of rods lashed together and wrapped with soft buckskin. The cradle could be carried as shown here or slung on the side of the saddle when moving camp. Mothers were extremely proud of the decoration on their babies' cradles and amongst many of the Plains, Plateau and Woodland tribes elaborate beadwork covered the tops and sides of such cradles.

Amongst these tribes it was the custom to hang trinkets and amulets as moving attractions for the baby and the Navajo would use pieces of colored shell, berries and pieces of turquoise.

Navajo

Athabaskan language family.

This old man, Hoshkay Yazhie, photographed in about 1920 by Guy C. Cross, is wearing a typical turquoise necklace as well as a harness-leather bandolier decorated with silver buttons. His skin and cloth cap, again decorated with buttons and with a bunch of turkey feathers on the crown, is probably one of the modern versions of an ancient animal-skin cap associated with war.

The Navajo had migrated southwards from their northern homes, arriving in the central southern part of present-day Colorado and northern New Mexico in the middle of the sixteenth century. Here they found Spanish horses and sheep, whose wool was being used for weaving by the Pueblo people, and it is assumed that they learnt their weaving skills from those ancient pueblo dwellers. Becoming gradually stronger from their raids for horses into the Spanish settlements and into the pueblos for sheep and goats, they followed their growing flocks and, searching for new sources of plunder, took up a nomadic life style. After the United States gained New Mexico from the Spanish in 1846 the Navajo were a continual nuisance with their raiding until finally subdued by Colonel Kit Carson. A large portion of the tribe was rounded up and forcibly marched over 300 miles (480km) - still remembered as 'The Long March' during which many suffered - to Fort Sumner in 1864. There they were held prisoners for some years, many dying of starvation and disease in that dry land. It was not until 1869 that they were allowed to return to their homelands where they finally became settled as they are today.

Pima

River, Bajo and Sobaipuri Pimans. Uto-Aztecan language family

*T*his good-looking Pima girl is called Lieta. She is dressed in her best for her portrait by Frank Russell on the Gila Reservation, Sacaton, Arizona, in 1902, and has her face painted in an ancient and outdated fashion which was probably reconstructed especially for the photographer. Painting was an ancient form of decoration and a baby's face was painted soon after birth with red ochre mixed with his mother's milk, which was supposed to improve the skin. Later the paint was applied mixed with grease to prevent chapping. Face and body paint was used by men and women and was supposed to 'symbolize the thought or fancy of the artist.' The custom had completely died out by the time Russell photographed Lieta and 'it was with difficulty that two persons could be hired to paint the faces that the writer might photograph them.'

Tattooing was also a popular decoration in the early days and it was said that the tattoo lines prevented wrinkles and kept them looking youthful, the original meanings of the designs having been lost long ago.

The ancestors of the A-A-Tam, or The People, as they called themselves, are said to have settled in the Salt River valley in ancient times and built irrigation canals and reservoirs and large adobe pueblos, the remains of which can still be seen. Their decline was probably attributable to constant harassment by various tribes such as the Apache; however, in spite of this and later problems over water and land rights, they have survived today and live on reservations at Salt River and Gila.

Zia Pueblo

Keresan language family

A man from the town of Zia, an isolated pueblo situated on the Jemez River, a tributary of the Rio Grande, some 30 miles (48km) north of present-day Albuquerque, New Mexico. He appears to be wearing a trade blanket rather than the traditional native weaving when photographed by T. Harmon Parkhurst in 1935. In the blasé cities of the east at that time the Southwest was looked on as a backward area, unequal in intelligence or resources, its people stifled by their Indian and Spanish heritage. But to the artists who drifted down to Santa Fe and the surrounding country it was a fresh new experience, and not the least of this freshness can be put down to the Indians of the area. So different to the debased and poverty-ridden people of the reservations, these Indians had so far been able to maintain some dignity, and in their colorful dress were ideal models for these art-hungry easterners.

The Zia are the descendants of a once large pueblo known as Old Zia. They joined in the Pueblo Revolt against the Spanish oppressors in 1680, but in 1692 they were once again under Spanish rule. They suffered a great setback and a large part of the tribe was destroyed, with the remainder baptized and converted to Catholicism. Although tribal numbers were at an all-time low, they recovered and today Zia is a thriving community.

At one time the Zia were an agricultural people farming along the river bottoms by their pueblo, but today, although a certain amount of farming is still carried on, they are more of a pastoral people tending large herds of sheep, goats, horses and cattle.

The Plains

ARAPAHO • ARIKARA • ASSINIBOIN
BLACKFEET • CHEYENNE • COMANCHE • CROW
GROS VENTRE • HIDATSA • IOWA • KANSA
KIOWA • KITSAI • LIPAN APACHE • MANDAN
MISSOURIA • OMAHA • PLAINS OJIBWA • OSAGE
OTO • PAWNEE • PONCA • QUAPAW • SARCEE
SIOUX • TONKAWA • WICHITA

*G*eographically the Great Plains covers the vast area from what are now the provinces of Alberta, Saskatchewan and Manitoba in Canada, south to Arkansas, Texas and New Mexico in the United States. Marking a quite specific barrier in the west is the massive range of the Rocky Mountains and the Mississippi and Missouri rivers in the east. Within these boundaries lies what the early white visitors believed to be a desert, for they saw farming as virtually impossible owing to the arid climate, the searing winds and terrible storms plus the many crop pests. To them it was fit only for cattle and once the buffalo had been eliminated room was available for cows and, later, sheep. To the Indians living on the periphery but being forced into the Plains by encroaching settlement and neighboring tribes it became an ideal land for their non-agricultural and, with the acquisition of the horse, nomadic existence. In those early days it was a paradise for a hunting people. Enormous herds of buffalo darkened the Plains for miles and were intermingled with vast numbers of antelope, elk and deer all feeding on the lush indigenous grasses. The skies were filled with innumerable flocks of birds, while bears, wolves, cougars and many smaller mammals roamed the woods and valleys. Faced with the inexorable advance of white settlement the Plains tribes were forced into almost continual warfare, culminating in their defeat.

Taken by William S. Soule in the mid-nineteenth century there is some confusion over the title of this picture; it is in the collection twice, once as 'Kicking Bird's camp' and again as 'Lone Wolf's camp'. Both men were Kiowa chiefs and what is indisputable is the typical nature of this camp site, probably near Fort Sill.

Arapaho

Northern and Southern Arapaho. Algonquian language family.

*T*his photograph by Soule is believed to shows the sons of Little Raven of the Arapaho, one of the chiefs of the Inunaine or Our People, but as in many Soule photographs there is some doubt over the labeling of the picture, and although the man on the left is almost certainly Little Bear, one of Little Raven's sons, the man on the right is purported to be Shield and may not be a son but rather a nephew.

Little Raven was born in 1820 and, although he gained his chieftainship through his exploits as a warrior, was generally friendly to the whites and signed the Medicine Lodge Treaty in 1867.

The clothing and ornaments are interesting in that the figure on the left wears long dentalium-shell earrings of the type often worn by women. He also sports a fine silver trade gorget and holds an eagle feather fan. Both men are wearing large scoop-shaped finger rings.

Originally a sedentary agricultural people living in northern Minnesota, the Arapaho moved gradually southwest and allied themselves with the Cheyenne who were also on the move. They appear to have separated into two bands before 1840, the Northern group settling around the North Platte River and the Southern group continuing on down toward the Arkansas River. They are thus now on reservations in these same areas: the Northern Arapaho sharing a reservation at Wind River, Wyoming, with the Shoshone and the Southern Arapaho in Oklahoma together with the Cheyenne.

THE PLAINS
Assiniboin

Siouan language family.

The Assiniboin - or Stoney as they are called in Canada - are of the Siouan family closely related to the Yanktonai, or Nakota. Their first contact with whites placed them around Lake Winnipeg about 1640. During the historic period they gradually moved south and west and, having acquired horses in the middle of the eighteenth century, they became fully-fledged nomadic Plains Indians until they were settled on their present reservations: Fort Belknap, between the Milk River and the Little Rockies in western Montana, and Fort Peck, which they share with the Yanktonai, on the Missouri River in eastern Montana. In Canada the largest reservation is probably that at Morley, near Calgary in Alberta.

These men - Horse Boy and Boy Chief - were photographed by William H. Jackson at Fort Belknap in about 1908. They are wearing their best clothes, as it would appear from the picture that some sort of ceremony has taken, or is about to take, place.

They are both wearing extremely fine skin shirts with beaded shoulder and arm strips, the shirt on the left has typical hourglass Blackfoot designs whilst the other one is of the Crow pattern with large blocks of color. Both shirts are copiously fringed with ermine. Horse Boy is holding a feather banner which appears to be decorated with peacock feathers.

Cheyenne

Northern and Southern Cheyenne. Algonquian language family.

Unfortunately this fine portrait of Wolf Robe by De Lancy Gill from 1909 shows this handsome Southern Cheyenne man only in white man's clothes apart from the coup feathers in his hair, a silver scarf slide at his throat and a bandolier with brass stud decoration.

He also wears a peace medal which it is not possible to identify in this picture. Little is known of this man but he was undoubtedly a warrior and is mentioned as having taken part in a skirmish with troops prior to the ghastly massacre at Sand Creek in 1864.

Living before 1700 as an agricultural people in what is now Minnesota, the Cheyenne were driven gradually westwards by pressure from the Sioux tribes, who were themselves being pressed by the Chippewa who had already acquired guns. By 1804 Lewis and Clark found them in the Black Hills of present-day South Dakota, from where they drifted west and south. In the 1830s a part of the tribe moved to the Arkansas River while the remainder eventually settled around the headwaters of the North Platte and Yellowstone rivers. Having moved onto the Plains they acquired all the Plains' traits and became true nomadic hunters following the buffalo until, forced by the ever advancing frontier, they allied with the Sioux and Arapaho and became prominent in most of the wars on the frontier. They now live on reservations in Montana and Oklahoma.

Comanche

Uto-Aztecan language family.

The girl on the left, pictured in 1891, is the daughter of the great Comanche chief Quanah Parker, the son of a chief who married a captive white woman named Cynthia Anne Parker. Quanah and his Kwahadi band were inveterate raiders along the Texas border and he refused to sign the Medicine Lodge Treaty in 1867, continued his raiding, and was one of the leaders in the attack at Adobe Walls in 1874.

His group were the last Comanche fighters to surrender to the US Army. Being still a young man, and possibly because of his part-white ancestry, he found it less traumatic to tread the white man's road. He arranged for the leasing of reservation land, the setting up of schools and encouraged house building and agricultural programs. At the same time he did not discard his own native ceremonies and beliefs. For many years he was an influential figure in dealing with the government on behalf of his people. He spoke English and Spanish as well as his own native tongue and lived in a large comfortable house surrounded by fields, where he died in 1911.

The fine native dresses worn by the girls show the traditional southern Plains use of simply-decorated skin dresses with plenty of fringing.

Comanche

Uto-Aztecan language family.

*U*nsure of their fate at the hands of the white man this frightened woman and her children have been persuaded to pose for this sad picture by William S. Soule in 1873. Their dress appears to be mostly of white manufacture, the blankets probably being trade items, the center one is of the Hudson's Bay type with one black stripe. They have retained their undecorated moccasins. The Comanche - once regarded as 'The Lords of the Southern Plains' - were the only tribe of Shoshonean stock living entirely on the Plains; they were true nomadic people known for their fantastic horsemanship. They were always at war with the early Spanish invaders but were generally friendly to most Americans except the Texans, against whom they carried on a fierce and relentless war for forty years. With the signing of the Medicine Lodge Treaty in 1867 they were finally settled on a reservation in Oklahoma. Never a large tribe, they were decimated by their wars and disease, and those remaining today are well mixed with the blood of Mexicans and Spaniards as well as that of the other Oklahoma Indian tribes with whom they now live.

Crow

River and Mountain Crow. Siouan language family.

The Crow, although always friendly to the whites, were constantly at war with their neighbors the Sioux, Cheyenne and Blackfeet. It was mostly in a defensive role, but many feats of bravery were achieved by their chiefs and warriors. Aleek-chea-ahoosh, or Plenty Coups, gained his name by obtaining such honors (coups) and there is a story that shows the respect given to a man who was able to sport such honors. The Crow had been subjected to a petty indignity by an ill-advised missionary, the occurrence being the last in a long line of attacks on their customs, and feelings were running high when a Council was called where young warriors made stirring speeches, working their listeners up until they were ready to fight. But now a big, square-jawed man arose and made a short speech full of plain good sense. His speech could not compare with that of the others, having neither the fire nor words, he did not even have popular sympathy, and yet he quelled the disturbance in those few words: 'As I looked it dawned on me the reason for his power. While the gifted speaker of the big words wore only a single untufted feather in his hair the other man had eagle feathers all round his head and trailing down his back and two feet along the ground, I knew then that I was listening to the voice of Plenty Coups and realised how a few words from a man of deeds will go further than all the stirring speeches of one who has no record of prowess to back up his threats.'

THE PLAINS
Crow

River and Mountain Crow. Siouan language family.

There is a poignancy about these proud figures, the finery of their native attire replaced by the almost beggarly look of white man's clothing. These men are, however, still wearing beaded moccasins, invariably one of the last pieces of native dress to be replaced by so-called civilized clothes. From left to right, these people are: Etchci-re-kash-cha-racha or Poor Elk, Kam-de-wat-se or Blackfoot, A-pats-ke or Long Ears, I-sa-sush or He Shows his Face, and Mit-cno-ash or Onion. Whether all the men in the picture are chiefs is problematical but there is no doubt about Blackfoot, second chief of the Mountain Crow and a famous man in his time. Apart from being an impressively tall (6ft 3in) and muscular figure, he was a great orator and leader of his people. In 1868 he was prominent at the Fort Laramie Treaty meeting which set boundaries for his tribe. He died in 1877. The Crow people called themselves Absaroka, or Children of the Long-Beaked Bird. At one time they were united with the Hidatsa and lived in the upper Missouri River country, but a split occured sometime in the sixteenth century and the Crow moved into the area of the Rocky Mountains of Montana. In the early eighteenth century a further division occurred into the Mountain and River people, and one band settled along the Yellowstone and Missouri river areas whilst the others stayed close to the mountains of Montana and Wyoming. The hostility of neighboring enemy tribes meant they seemed in danger of being exterminated, but they survived to become middlemen and great traders and whilst there were some disagreements the Crow were generally peaceful towards the whites and joined with them to subdue their most powerful enemies, the Sioux.

THE PLAINS
Kiowa

Aztec-Tanoan language family.

A young man of some wealth judging by the size of his breastplate - a prestige item of decoration throughout the Plains area, and on the southern Plains such ornaments were more often of a smaller size. He has one otter skin and one trade cloth wrapping around his braids and he carries a bandolier-style bowcase and quiver. These breastplates were never intended as armor but were merely decorative. The origin of the so called 'hair pipe' goes back to prehistoric times when a tubular bead, probably made of shell, was used as a hair decoration by the eastern Indians. These beads were made from the central column of the conch shell and it, and the resultant bead, became a trade item, finding their way across to the Plains. By the middle of the seventeenth century a glass substitute made in Europe was introduced to the Indians of the eastern woodlands by white traders, and a few silver and brass tubular beads were also available.
The name 'hair pipe' seems to have come into use about this time when shell pipes were being used by some men as hair decorations. They were either threaded through a cord and hung on either side of the head in front of the ears or threaded through a lock of hair and worn high on each side of the forehead. Shell hair pipes were found to be impractical for the many uses to which they were put because they were so fragile and were continually breaking. It was this that prompted the introduction of the bone hair pipe. A trader noticed Indians wearing corn-cob pipe stems strung together and used as breast ornaments, so they set up a factory to make these new bone hair pipes which today have progressed from bone to plastic.
The specimen worn by Koi-khan-hole in this Soule photograph shows the transition from shell to bone as the majority of the pipes appear to be of shell with just a few bone ones.

Osage

Siouan language family.

This Osage man, Governor Joe, is wearing a Peace Medal and his body carries the tribal 'mark of honor' signified by the tattooing which was placed upon selected warriors to ensure they were faithful in keeping the ancient rituals.

The Osage, or Wazhazhe, are one of the most important of the southern Siouan groups and are sometimes referred to as Dhegiha. They were at one time closely related to the Omaha, Ponca, Kansa and Quapaw, living as a single body along the Ohio River. They were a farming people living in permanent villages in wooden houses, but they also made use of buffalo and other game in hunting forays out onto the Plains. There they came into contact with some of the southern Plains tribes and territorial fights ensued.

The Osage allied themselves with the French in 1714 and were held in terror by the neighboring tribes, but in 1808 they signed a treaty with the United States and ceded most of their lands. The limits of their territory were set in 1870 in Oklahoma where they live today. The tribe possessed funds in the US Treasury and the income from this, together with leases from grazing rights and the rights to oil and minerals on the reservation, made them, at that time, the richest tribe in the United States.

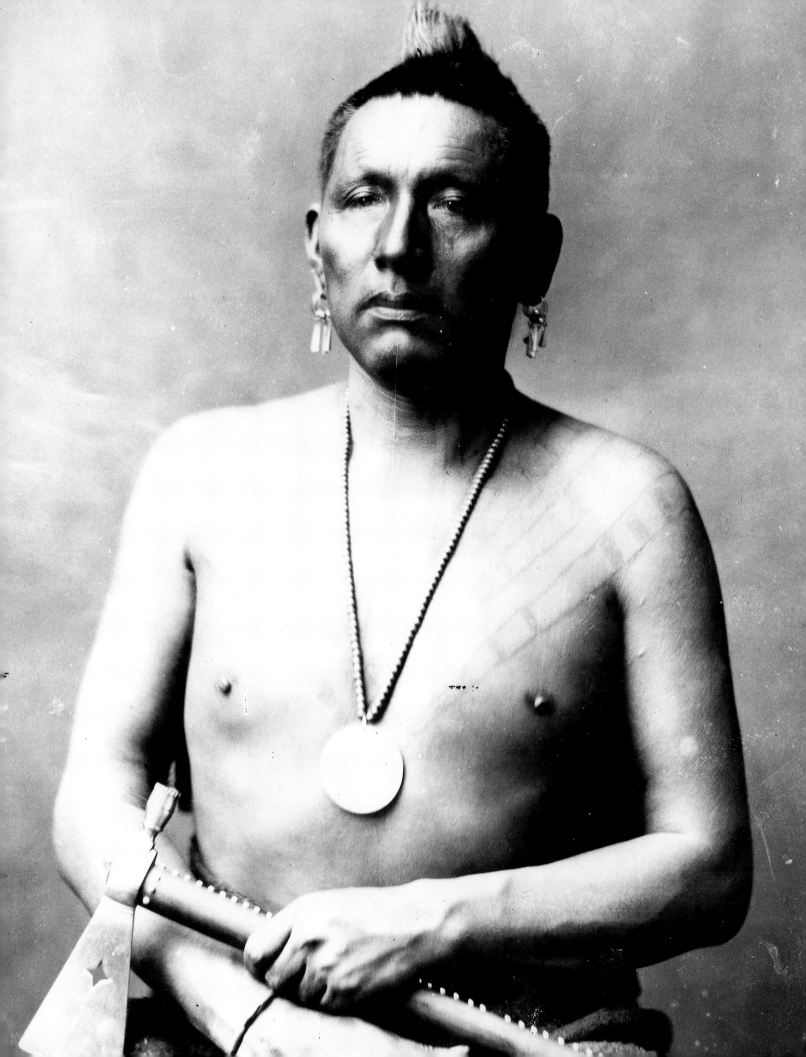

Pawnee

Skiddi , Pitahauerat, Chani and Kithahki Pawnee.
Caddoan language family.

A stereograph picture, probably taken by Gardiner, of a wild-looking Kihahki or Republican Pawnee warrior wearing a buffalo robe. The man is called Esteemed Son. As the West became more settled there was a great demand for views of the scenery, and pictures of Indians were also extremely popular. These stereoscopic photographs were made to view through a machine rather like binoculars which produced a three-dimensional effect. The Pawnee called themselves Chahiksichaniks, or Men of Men. They were village people occupying the valley of the Platte River in what is today Nebraska. They grew a variety of beans, corn, and squashes and, because of their central position on the Plains, they were also hunters of buffalo and other game. As early as the seventeenth century the Pawnee were raiding into New Mexico to procure horses and the Spanish authorities there spent two centuries unsuccessfully trying to bring peace to the area. In spite of continuing pressure from settlement in their own lands the Pawnee were generally peaceable to the whites and showed great forbearance under much provocation. In fact they formed a famous regiment of scouts under Major North and saw service throughout the Plains' wars. The Pawnee had a rich ceremonial life, much of which centered around the heavens and the stars, particularly the Morning and Evening stars. Many of the complicated ceremonies concerned extraordinary medicine bundles with their connected rituals. At one time they practiced human sacrifice in connection with their star beliefs, a rare event amongst American Indians of the historic period. The opening of immigrant trails through Pawnee country during the 1840s introduced disease and decimation, reducing their population so drastically that they were unable to defend themselves from their traditional enemies the Sioux. What lands they had not been forced to cede to the government were opened to white settlement in the late 1800s and the remnants of the Pawnee were moved to Oklahoma where they can be found today.

Sioux

Mdewakanton, Sisseton, Teton, Wahpekute, Wahpeton, Yankton and Yanktonai Sioux. Siouan language family.

A member of the Hunkpapa band of the Teton Sioux, also called the Lakota, Tatanka Yotanka or Sitting Bull became one of the best known Indian figures of the frontier West. Of lowly birth, Sitting Bull became a great fighter and warrior but in later life tended to use his great powers as a healer and medicine man. It was he who told his people in that great gathering of tribes prior to the Custer battle that he had dreamt of 'soldiers with their hats off falling into camp.' His people took this to be a prophecy of victory and so it turned out when General Custer and his entire command of two hundred and fifty men were killed at the Battle of the Little Big Horn in 1876. Following this great victory Sitting Bull and his people fled to Canada but they were forced to return and Sitting Bull surrendered at Fort Buford in 1881. He spent many subsequent years of his life working on behalf of his people but died tragically at his home on the Standing Rock Reservation in December 1890.

THE PLAINS
Sioux

Mdewakanton, Sisseton, Teton, Wahpekute, Wahpeton, Yankton and Yanktonai Sioux. Siouan language family.

From left to right these men attending a council of chiefs at Fort Laramie in 1868 are: Spotted Tail, Roman Nose, Man Afraid of His Horses, Lone Horn, Whistling Elk, Pipe, and Slow Bull.

In the spring of 1868 representatives of the Sioux, Cheyenne and Arapaho went to Fort Laramie to try and conclude a peace following the so-called Red Cloud War. The eventual signing of the treaty was a victory for Red Cloud and left an uneasy peace on the frontier.

This fascinating photograph by Alexander Gardner is exceptional in its 'unposed' setting. It is interesting to note that most of the men wear shirts, blankets and heavy winter buffalo robes whilst Pipe sits, unconcernedly, bare to the waist! Three men wear beautifully decorated porcupine-quill shirts and Spotted Tail, on the left, wears a hair ornament of prized metal discs which are attached to the scalp lock and fall to the ground in decreasing sizes. These old warriors were all names to conjure with in their day, they all had fine war records in battles with other tribes and the white man, and they were probably proud to have their portraits taken on such an occasion.

The translation of many Indian names tried the best of interpreters and Man Afraid of His Horses is a good example. His name was impossible to put into a few concise words but a more probable, but obviously unusable translation, would be Man of Whose Horses People are Afraid. Most of the other names would have had a meaning to their owners who could, and did, change them throughout their lives.

Sioux

Mdewakanton, Sisseton, Teton, Wahpekute, Wahpeton, Yankton and Yanktonai Sioux. Siouan language family.

*T*his portrait by David F. Barry shows the great Hunkpapa war chief Gall, or Pizi, photographed at Fort Buford in 1881 draped in a buffalo robe and holding a circular feather fan. Born in 1840, Gall was a warrior of some note - another name of his was The Man Who Goes in the Middle - but he really came to fame as an outstanding general with his handling of his warriors at the Battle of the Little Big Horn in June 1876.
Because the Sioux were such a large group, and each part was being harassed by pressures from the advancing frontier and the US Army, there was always much dissension and disharmony amongst the leading families and head men and this was probably the basis for the split between Gall and Sitting Bull in later years. Gall was in attendance at the inauguration of Sitting Bull as chief of all the Sioux but other prominent men did not concur to this arrangement and such men as Spotted Tail and Red Cloud were keen to sign peace agreements with the whites.
Following the Custer battle Gall fled to Canada with Sitting Bull but withdrew from his following and surrendered to Major Iles at Poplar River in 1881. He settled at Standing Rock and, possibly due in some part to the influence of the Agent, James McLaughlin, who had no love for Sitting Bull, he proceeded to vilify Sitting Bull whilst he himself became the 'white man's friend.' He was later an influential figure much esteemed for his work for his people. He died in 1894.

Plateau and Basin

PLATEAU: CAYUSE • COEUR D'ALÊNE COLVILLE • FLATHEAD • KALISPEL • KLAMATH KLICKITAT • KOOTENAI • LILLOOET • MOLALA NEZ PERCE • NICOLA • OKANAGAN • PALUS SANPOIL • SENIJEXTEE • SHUSWAP • SPOKANE TENINO • THOMPSON • UMATILLA • WALLA WALLA • WASCO • WISHRAM • YAKIMA BASIN: BANNOCK • CHEMEHUEVI • MONO PAIUTE • SHOSHONI • UTE • WASHOE

Backing onto the Great Plains in the east , onto the desert and the Pueblo people in the south , bordering the 'Totem Pole' people to the north and the lowlands of the Californian coastline to the west, the Plateau area is a land of patchy mountainous forests and deep lush valleys and meadowlands, with two great river systems, the Fraser and the Columbia. On the southern edge the land runs into the Great Basin, a huge area of semi-desert and of grassland interspersed with deeply-carved canyons. The dominant river in this part is the Colorado, cutting across the center and twisting its way through the depths of the Grand Canyon.

The people of the Great Basin led a fairly spartan subsistence existence. On the northern Plateau land, however, a rich culture existed. There was plenty of game, the rivers provided a wealth of fish, whilst fruit and vegetables grew in the grassy meadows, and many trade patterns were developed with the Plains peoples to the east and the coastal tribes in the northwest.

The photograph shows the band camp of the easternmost division of the Shoshone, named after their chief Washakie, or Shoots the Buffalo Running, who was of mixed Shoshoni and Umatilla blood. The Shoshoni were divided on a geographival basis: Northern, Eastern and Western.

Nez Perce

Upper and Lower Nez Perce. Shahaptian language family.

Born about 1840, of mixed Nez Perce and Cayuse blood, he was given the name Joseph by the missionary Henry Spalding. His Nez Perce name is Hein-mot Too-ya-la-kekt, or Thunder Rolling Over the Mountains This photograph was taken in about 1901 by Lee Moorhouse.

The Nez Perce, living in what were to become Idaho, eastern Oregon and Washington, were a peaceable and intelligent tribe and it was Joseph's boast that up to the war of 1877 the Nez Perce had never killed a white man. A traditional aboriginal domain of the people was the Wallowa Valley in Oregon and this land had been guaranteed to the tribe for ever by government treaty. In 1875, however, the land was opened for settlement and the people were forced to move. Such a move could have been carried out peaceably, though with great reluctance, but for the murder of some white settlers by furious young men of the tribe and Joseph, the new chief, was virtually forced to go on the warpath. The story of the flight of the Nez Perce, in an attempt to reach peace and safety in Canada, has been compared to that of Xenophon's Ten Thousand, and the generalship of Joseph to that of Napoleon. Against almost overwhelming odds he was finally forced to surrender when only 50 miles (80 km) from the Canadian border.

Promises were made to Joseph and his few remaining people that they could return to their beloved valley but these promises were soon broken and the remnants of a once proud people were sent to the infamous Indian Territory far from their old homes. They were finally allowed back, but not to their valley, and are now settled on reservations in Lapwai and Colville.

PLATEAU AND BASIN
Nez Perce

Upper and Lower Nez Perce. Shahaptian language family.

*D*ressed for display, this young woman, E-we-tone-my, wears a fully-beaded cape dress. She is using a typical high pommel and cantle woman's saddle, the pommel of which has a bead-decorated flap, but surprisingly her horse is undecorated. Attached at the back of the saddle are two parfleche containers with extra long fringes.

As horse-breeders the Nez Perce were surpassed by none. Their horses first reached them in about 1700 from the Shoshoni who had obtained them from the Spanish settlements of the Southwest. The Shoshoni, like the Nez Perce, traded outward toward the Crow and via them to the Missouri River tribes such as the Mandan and Hidatsa. The Nez Perce and their close neighbors the Palus had a liking for colored or Pinto horses and possibly this may have been the reason they practiced the gelding of their lesser stallions and those without color. They culled the yearly crop of foals and actually controlled the breeding of their best stallions and mares. Such customs must originally have come from the Spaniards and were practiced by a few tribes to a far lesser degree. The Nez Perce were the experts and it was said that horses gelded by them recovered quicker and suffered less than those of other tribes. One of the other great achievements of these people was the raising of the Appaloosa horse and their intelligent breeding of these and other fine horses produced animals of top quality for war and hunting, which of course made them of great trading value.

If for no other reason, the Nez Perce are today known as the best horse breeders in the northwest.

Nez Perce

Upper and Lower Nez Perce. Shahaptian language family.

This rather apprehensive looking boy is called Joseph Ratunda and he was photographed by Rodman Wanamaker in about 1900 wearing a Plains-style costume with otter skin wrapped braids and a bandolier made from the same skin with trade mirrors. He wears a deer-hair head roach and various necklaces of beads and an ermine skin. He has on Plains fully-beaded moccasins and his beaded wristlets show stylized floral beadwork patterns more typical of the Plateau area style.

As the followers of Joseph drifted back to their own country from their exile in Indian Territory, some of the warriors could not understand that their fighting days were over and they still liked to boast of past deeds. Much of this old warlike spirit stirred the hearts of the young men and it was with difficulty that the agents were able to handle these problems. Mostly it was done by rigorously forcing the young men to give up any of the old tribal affiliations, and to discard the old ceremonies and beliefs. Young boys had their hair cut off and were forced into the uncomfortable white man's clothes.

It was a time of trauma for all the people and drunkenness was another ever-present problem punishable with a jail sentence and a fine of a horse, which was sold to supply the culprit with rations.

Thankfully the days are gone when it was the policy to suppress Indian culture and today such a boy as the one in the picture is able to wear traditional clothing and take part in dances in almost the old way.

Shoshoni

Eastern, Northern, and Western Shoshoni. Shoshonean language family.

These five Shoshoni men and one small boy are dancers of the Grass Dance, a Plains-derived dance. They were pictured on the Fort Hall Reservation, Idaho, in about 1900, and are wearing an incredible assortment of clothing showing influences from the Plains and Great Lakes areas.

The man on the left wears his hair in the swept-up Crow style and he has a dentalium shell choker around his neck. He wears a white man's cloth shirt, suspended from the neck of which is a loom-beaded pendant. He also wears two brass arm bands. His leggings are beaded in typical Plains style, as are his moccasins. The fine bandolier bag worn over his shoulder is typical of the Great Lakes area of the eastern woodlands, as is the beaded apron he wears. Such loom-beaded bags as this, and also the two worn by the second man, may have been acquired in trade or as gifts, although it is difficult to see how or where people from so far apart could have met.

The second man appears to have painted his forehead with white clay and has also used it to hold his front hair in place. Over the two crossed bandolier bags he wears a Plains loop necklace, probably made of beads. Again his leggings are decorated with typical Plains-style beaded strips. His beaded and fringed apron is typical of the finest Chippewa work. The middle man also wears a loop necklace and appears to be wearing 'Long Johns,' often decreed for modesty by Victorian whites. His breechclout is similar in style to that of the first man and must have come from the Prairie people of the east.

The other two men appear to be wearing more typical Shoshoni-style clothing, the man on the left with a traditional hair 'bang.'

Shoshoni

Eastern, Northern, and Western Shoshoni. Shoshonean language family.

This fine portrait from 1899 shows Weason, a young Shoshoni man who has partly adopted white man's clothing and yet still kept some of his traditional decorations. He wears a bone-bead loop necklace which were popular amongst many of the tribes, particularly those on the Plateau and northern Plains. His blanket appears to be of Southwestern origin and was probably acquired through trade. He wears his hair in the 'pompadour' style rather similar to that used by the Crow but also popular amongst Shoshoni, Bannock and Ute men. Like most Indians, the Shoshoni were proud of their long black hair and often wore it loose on one side and wrapped, usually with otter skin, on the other side, as in the picture which was taken in Denver by Rose and Hopkins.

Shoshoni lives were varied: those of the more northerly and easterly groups were typical of the Plains' buffalo-hunting culture, while to the west the land was almost barren and the people lived virtually a subsistence life on fish, small game and roots, seeds and nuts.

Today they live on reservations in Nevada, Idaho and in Wyoming, which they share with their former enemies the Arapaho.

Umatilla

Shahaptian language family.

Standing in front of a rare buffalo-hide teepee this old warrior is called Shut-a-mo-ne or Sheep Cross Horns. He is of mixed Yakima and Umatilla blood and wears the costume of his Umatilla uncle who is reputed to have killed a Bannock chief and taken his head to General Howard of the US Army.

He wears a beautiful outfit with ermine skin and shaved horn bonnet. His shirt shows the distinct Crow-style beadwork whilst his moccasins are decorated in the floral Plateau style. His loop necklace has abalone shell discs on either side.

Both the Yakima and the Umatilla are tribes of the Shahaptian language group which takes in most of the Plateau people, these particular tribes living in present day Oregon and Washington. They were semi-Plains tribes, having agricultural lands but venturing across the Rockies to hunt buffalo on the Plains. They adopted much of the Plains styles of clothing, exaggerating some parts of it as can be seen by the exceptionally wide beaded strips on the leggings of the Shut-a-mo-ne in the photograph.

All these people were great horseowners and, living as they did west of the Rockies, they were not subjected to continual horse raids, and the much milder climate produced good feeding for their large herds.

Today these people live on reservations in eastern Oregon and Washington.

Ute

**Uintah, Yampa, and Uncompahgre Utes. Uto-Aztecan
language family.**

*C*alled by their neighbors the Blue Sky People,' the
Utes were a warlike people occupying what is now
Colorado and the eastern part of Utah. Having acquired
horses as early as the 1600s they became like Plains Indians
except that, unlike most Plains people they ate fish as well
as berries, nuts, seeds and various roots.
The photograph from 1870, probably posed, shows a man
wearing nothing but a breechclout and this would be what
a typical warrior would look like. He has a bowcase and
quiver, with a large part- beaded flap, slung over his
shoulder. One of the Plains' traits taken up by the Utes
appears in their dress clothing worn for ceremonial
occasions. They used large amounts of beadwork of the
finest work as well as exaggerated decorations of many
descriptions, giving them a very elegant style. They were
also adept at transforming the white man's clothes with
Plains' items, resulting in some exciting combinations.

California

ACHUMAWI • CAHTO • CAHUILLA • CHUMASH
COLUSA • CONCHO • COSTANOAN • CUPENO
DIEGUENO • FERNANDENO • GABRIELINO
HUPA • JUANENO • KAROK • KITTANEMUK
KONKOW • LASSIK • LUISENO • MAIDU • MIWOK
MODOC • MONO • NOMLAKI • PATWIN • POMO
SALINAN • SERREN • SHASTA • SERRANO
TAKELMA • WAPPO • WASHO • WINTU • WIYOT
YANA • YOKUTS • YUKI • YUROK

*H*istorians and anthropologists have called the
northern parts of the California culture area a
'pale reflection' of the vibrant northwest coast culture
with which it merges. The southern parts reflected, in a
small way, some of the Southwest's traits, but in the
center, where the climate was temperate and the land
rather barren, it was an easygoing rather backward
lifestyle. Although there were animals to hunt, much of
their time was spent in the gathering of seeds, acorns,
berries, roots and vegetables, as well as fishing. The
Spaniards were the first to arrive and by 1796 they had set
up a series of missions throughout the area, their
apathetic converts becoming known as 'Mission' Indians.
The California peoples were generally non-aggressive and
there was little in the way of warlike opposition to
settlement; in fact these harmless people were continually
harassed by the white community. The only major conflict
was the Modoc War of 1872-73, when a band of Modoc
led by Kintpuash, or Captain Jack, resisted their
confinement to reservations and held off the US Army
from a base in the Lava Beds for many months, inflicting
some serious losses. They finally surrendered; the leaders
were hanged and the rest relocated to Indian Territory.

A Pomo fisherman in his very distinctive boat made of bound
rushes or tule; also in the boat is a conical basket used for
catching and holding fish. Because of the abundance of reeds
and rushes in this area the Pomo used it in many ways -
clothing, matting, and housing, as well as boatbuilding.

CALIFORNIA
Hupa

Athabascan language family.

A people of the northwestern part of California, the Hupa subsisted mostly on fish such as salmon and sea trout, as well as acorns and other fruits of the forests. The hunting of deer was carried out to a lesser extent and, unlike most other Californian tribes, they did not eat birds of any sort because of religious taboos. They lived in wooden houses, the floors of which were below ground. Away from home on hunting or fishing trips, or when harvesting, they would build brush shelters which gave sufficient cover in the generally dry climate.

This photograph of the Hupa Jumping Dance was probably taken by A.W. Ericson in 1893 and shows the distinctive headband used, with variations, in several dances. Some dances were associated with the display of wealth and others were for religious purposes. The so-called Jumping Dance and the White Deerskin Dance were held to help ward off all disasters and to regenerate the people for the coming new year. They usually lasted ten days and were held at the end of the summer. In the Jumping Dance the male-only dancers wore these elaborate headbands and carried basket-type 'wands' filled with dried grass or straw to keep their shape, all of which constituted a display of wealth.

These headbands are unique to this area and show considerable skill in their construction. The feathers in this particular style are those of the red and yellow woodpecker which were sewn to a buckskin backing or woven into a cloth made of milkweed. Because of the difficulties in obtaining the raw materials for them, and the time and skill in the construction, such outfits only belonged to the wealthy and were displayed with some pride during dances.

A. W. ERICSON.

Hupa

Athabascan language family.

*T*he people of California, or rather the women there, were famed for their exquisite basketry work; men only produced some coarse-twined examples such as fish traps. Different regions produced distinctly different designs and constituent materials, creating an abundance of diverse types from California's many different cultures.

In addition to that, every basket was itself unique and identifiable as the product of a specific individual, so the variety can only be imagined.

Women's baskets in the northwestern region where the Hupa lived were often finely twined from hazel or willow shoots and conifer root, overlaid externally with patterns in colored fern stems and grasses. Such everyday items as mush bowls would be made from twined conifer roots on a foundation of hazel sticks, embellished with a horizontal band of design in something like shiny yellow bear grass.

Women also wove dress caps and these could be ornamented further still with black maidenhair fern stem and woodwardia fern stem dyed to a rust color with alder bark. Very highly prized caps might have an additional overlay of dyed porcupine quills to provide a striking contrast.

This Hupa woman is believed to be a Mrs Freddy who was photographed by Pliny E. Goddard in 1902. She is pouring water from a basket cup into acorn meal being leached in a hollow in the sand. To her right is an acorn collecting basket. The importance of the acorn in the diet of so many of California's peoples could not be emphasized more clearly.

Karok

Hokan language family

A tribe from the northwest coast of California who lived along the Klamath River and whose culture and way of life closely resembled that of their near neighbors the Yurok and Hupa. In fact, many sources refer to them as being indistinguishable in appearance and customs from the Yurok.

Like some of the Northwest Coast tribes living above them, the display of wealth for prestige purposes was of high priority, but unlike these people they did not practice the Potlatch. The main status symbols were dentalium shells, colorful woodpecker scalps and beautifully-fashioned obsidian spear or knife blades, the actual possession and display of these objects was sufficient for the owner to receive respect and prestige.

Like all the other tribes of the California culture area, the Karok subsisted on the gathering of wild plant foods, the most important of which was probably the acorn. Fishing and the hunting of deer and elk, and a few bear, was carried out by the men. There was, however, a taboo concerning the eating of bear meat and salmon at the same time!

The people lived in plank houses which were partly underground. There were also separate so-called 'sweat' houses used by men only. Their clothing was a mixture of skins and vegetable fiber material, which was also used in the making of basketry hats and skirts for the women.

The photograph, taken prior to 1898, shows a man called Little Ike using what was known as a 'plunge' net, which was fixed to an oval-shaped frame and was dipped into the stream or river and the fish scooped out. Salmon was probably the most important fish, but trout, eels and other fish were also taken. Often a platform was erected on the bank of the river and a lifting net was used to catch them as they made their way upstream to spawn in the spring. Harpoons and gaffs were also used for fish and eels, as well as basketry fish traps across the smaller streams.

Pomo

Central, Eastern, Northern, Northwestern, Southern, and Southeastern Pomo. Hokan language family.

*T*his photograph, taken by C. Hart Merriam in 1907, shows Pomo dancers dressed for the Big Head Dance. Most of the tribes had secret societies whose functions were limitless, some being for war and some for religious purposes. The Big Head Dance was part of the Kuksu cult, which was a religious system involving the acquisition of spiritual power through direct contact with the spirit forces of the universe. This particular dance society held their performances in an earth-covered dance house and it involved the initiation of young boys into shamanistic roles.

The center figure in the photograph is the Big Head or Tuya, a male spirit. He is wearing a headdress based on a tule mat fastened over the head, possibly with a string hair net, and it is covered with feathers of owl and snow goose with the projecting feathers of the condor stripped of their vanes. These appear to be tipped with red woodpecker head feathers or the heads of red Californian poppy. They also sometimes used very small pieces of abalone shell.

The dancer also has white goose-feather bracelets and is wearing a skirt made of either shredded willow bark or the inner bark of the maple. The man on the right is wearing a headdress of crow or raven feathers with projecting sticks of willow or hazel shoots, which were often painted, and a collar of white goose feathers. He has on a cloth skirt and has a trailer of flicker feathers on a band of native hemp and tule. The left-hand figure has a headband of the same material and his belt is made in chequerboard fashion with bird scalps in alternating colors.

Such elaborate and unique costumes and accessories had been developed over hundreds of years and evolved from complicated rituals and religious beliefs.

The Northwest Coast

**ALSEANS • BELLA BELLA • BELLA COOLA
CHEHALIS • CHEMAKUM • CHINOOK
CLALLAM • COOS • DUWAMISH • EYAK
GITKSAN • HAIDA • HAISLA • KWAKIUTL
LUMMI • MAKAH • NUU-CHAH-NULTH
OOWEKEENO • QUILEUTE • QUINAULT
SALISH • SIUSLAWANS • SKOKOMISH
SWINOMISH • TLINGIT • TSIMSHIAN**

Dotted with small islands, the northwest coastline
runs from the northern tip of California some
1,500 miles (2,400km) north through British Columbia to
Alaska. It is bordered on the land side by the Cascade and
Rocky mountains. Because of its many islands, river
mouths, sounds, inlets and bays, this area is one of the
great fishing regions of the world and the livelihood of
the people of the area was mostly based on the sea.
In the southern parts of this area were tribes known as
traders of objects connected with the sea and others
that excelled in the making of fine baskets. The central
and northern areas were the centers of culture and,
because of the abundance of timber in the form of cedar,
it was inevitable that this material became so important in
their civilization. Here was a 'big' culture where people
hunted whales in wooden boats, lived in large houses
made from enormous cedar wood planks, carved religious
and mythological masks for their magical and exotic
ceremonies, and erected large, carved poles in honor of
their ancestors, and gave away their wealth in a prestige-
enhancing celebration known as the Potlatch.

*This photograph by G.M. Dawson shows the Haida settlement of
Skidegate on Queen Charlotte Island in 1878. It was named
after a succession of chiefs of that name. Note the canoes on the
shore, the houses, and the different poles and mortuary columns*

Coos

Penutian language family.

A small group of the most southerly of the Northwest Coast tribes living on the coastal strip of Oregon with the Rockies at their backs, the Coos subsisted mainly on the harvest of the sea in the form of seals, sea lions, salmon and shellfish, as well as the hunting of deer and elk inland in the spring where they also took salmon and other fish from the rivers and streams. Their houses, similar to others of the area, were built of cedar wood with gabled roofs, the floors being sunk in the ground. Although they made some small canoes, those of size and substance were traded from northern tribes.

The Native Americans were ingenious in the materials used for their clothing, from skins and furs of infinite variety, to native weavings of many sorts from grasses and fibers, including, as shown here in the photograph of the two girls from 1910, shredded bark and cattail. These outfits were made to shed the rain, as were others made of fur in this very wet area, and were probably worn over a skin skirt or dress. The youngest girl on the right is wearing a locally-made basketry hat and they are standing in front of a large upturned basket. The object held by the other girl could be a sort of wooden scythe with which to cut and hold reeds and rushes to be used in weavings and house coverings. The long strings of dentalium in the form of necklaces were obtained along the coastline and were a useful item of trade to people of the interior who valued them highly as decorations.

Although these people produced some fine basketry not much remains, for they were only a small group and on death their belongings were all broken and scattered over the grave.

Haida

Kaigani Haida and Haida. Na-Dene language family.

The making of baskets and basketry objects was practiced by many tribes in the United States but it reached perfection amongst the people of the Pacific Northwest Coast, California and the Southwest. The Tlingit and Haida were the chief basket makers of the northwest area.

Usually a basket was begun at the base in the weaver's lap but some weavers of the Haida, as in the photograph of the woman from Masset taken by Edward Allen in 1897, attach the beginnings of the basket to the top of a pole and work in an upside-down position. If the basket did not have native colored ingredients they were often painted with heraldic designs in red, black and blue.

Over years of evolution Indian women knew the best plants and materials for making good basketry and the constant search for, and husbanding of, the right type of plants was virtually a form of agriculture.

It was essential to harvest the material at the right time and to know how to dry and preserve it. There was an enormous variety in the process of producing basketry but the Haida and Tlingit seemed to have preferred the twined method as opposed to wrapping, coiling and the many other ingenious procedures. As well as the weaving of baskets Haida women also made hats, worn by people with their best decorative clothing on ceremonial occasions as a mark of their wealth. These hats were also known as Potlatch hats and were woven from split spruce roots as well as cedar bark and natural grasses. The designs painted on this rather distinctive form of headgear usually represented the owner's crest while most basketry designs were purely ornamental.

Kwakiutl

**Northern and Southern Kwakiutl. Wakashan
language family.**

*T*he Kwakiutl territory covered a large area north and
south of Queen Charlotte Straits in British
Columbia. They were basically a group of some thirty
smaller sub-tribes of which the Quatsino - to which Ma-Ma
Yockland pictured here belongs - are one. Today Quatsino
Sound is named after them and faces the Pacific Ocean on
the northern tip of Vancouver Island.

Living as they did on the coast these people had an almost
limitless supply of sea food which they exploited to the
full. Sea and inland fish were taken in nets and weirs and
there were annual trips to the herring spawning grounds
and the spring salmon runs. Clams, mussels, sea urchins
and barnacles were also harvested as well as inland
resources such as mountain sheep and goats and the
gathering of fruits and berries. Because of this abundance
of resources the people had leisure time to develop highly
technical skills in wood carving, particularly of masks
which were used in the various ceremonies and dances
connected with their rich mythological heritage. This rich
heritage gave rise to the Potlatch where wealthy people
beggared themselves by giving away huge quantities of
possessions to gain prestige.

Ma-Ma Yockland, pictured in 1912 by B.W. Leeson on
Vancouver Island, has a deformed head purposely
produced by applied pressure when she was a baby. Such a
practice was worldwide and known from ancient times,
sometimes as a mark of beauty or, as in this case, a mark of
distinction and superiority. This form of head deformation
is made by the application of bandages and pads applied
to the frontal bone thus giving a conical and elongated
shape to the head. It was practiced by these people as late
as the 1900s and apparently it had no ill effects of any sort
on the individual: the brain compensated for the
compression by extending to other areas of
least resistance.

Nun-chah-nulth

Wakashan language family.

*T*he mortuary shrine at Mowachaht of a chief, photographed by George Hunt in 1904, contains carvings of dead whalers. The skulls and effigies of whales were used in ceremonies that were believed to bring dead whales to the shore. These dead whales, which did occasionally get washed up on the shores, were a good source of oil, essential to the people, even if the meat was not too good! Because of the importance of whales in the subsistence of these people and the difficulties and danger attached to the killing of them, whalers were important people, usually chiefs, and were held in high esteem. Like most Indian people, those of the Northwest Coast believed in reincarnation so that death was not something to be feared. Upon his death, a wealthy man was laid out in his best clothes and surrounded by his wealth in the form of clothing, blankets and carvings - such as masks and hats as well as boxes and trunks - and thus he remained on show for several days. If not cremated, the body was then placed, usually in a squatting position, in a box and then in a small wooden house in the burial area, surrounded by mortuary poles carved with family crests. Another earlier method of burial was for the body to be placed in a mortuary column which had an inset burial chamber attached to it. Amongst some of the Salishan tribes bodies were placed in beautifully decorated canoes which were then hoisted up on posts or trees in a similar fashion to Plains' burials.

Following the death of a man of standing, a Death Potlatch would be held, during which all his possessions would be given away. Although the unique carvings of the northern and central Northwest Coast people reached an incredibly high standard the skills tended to diminish further south and the figures in the photograph appear crude compared to some of the great carvings produced by the Haida and Tlingit.

Tlingit

Coastal and Inland Tlingit. Na-Dene language family .

The photograph shows Inland Tlingit men and boys in 1895 in Potlatch dance costumes. The men are wearing shirts or jackets of wool, such shirts also being tailored in caribou or elk skin.

The foliate beadwork decoration is typical of these people whose culture tends to merge with that of the nearby Athabaskans. Both men and boys in the photograph are wearing an assortment of hats, the man in the center with a carved wooden front probably has it decorated with abalone and dentalium shells. One boy is wearing a special headdress of cut and worked mountain goat horns and all the men wear nose rings. The fine bags they wear are known as 'Octopus' bags because of the 'tentacles' or 'fingers' on the base. The young boy on the left of the picture is wearing an older type of shirt with a pointed bottom and half-oval join across the top, echoed in the later shirts as a line of beadwork. All the men are wearing face paint applied specially for the Potlatch dance.

The photographers, Winter and Pond, accidentally observed a Tlingit secret society dance and to avoid ethical problems were adopted into the tribe, and from this close association came many fine and intimate photographs. These people lived in villages or towns along the water fronts consisting usually of a long row of wooden houses with a conglomeration of mortuary and totem poles intermixed. Behind were the smoke houses in which the curing of salmon and other fish took place. During the summer most of these villages would be deserted when the people scattered out to fishing and hunting camps.

Although fishing was the most important means of subsistence a certain amount of inland hunting took place. Bears were killed for their meat, fat and skins, and deer, mountain sheep and goats also provided food and clothing. The Tlingit were also hunters of sea mammals such as seals, sea lions and porpoise which were killed with spears and harpoons.

Tlingit

Coastal and Inland Tlingit. Na-Dene language family.

These two Inland Tlingit men, Cou-Dah-Wot and Raven's Slave, were photographed in their ceremonial clothing.by Winter and Pond at Klukwan, Alaska, in about 1895. They are wearing typical elaborate ceremonial dress consisting of skin tunics of moose or caribou hide with designs, which in this case are probably heraldic rather than religious. Among the Tlingit, chiefs and wealthy men desired to proclaim their riches and such tunics probably belonged to aristocrats. These types of design are unique to this area and the figures, mostly animals, birds or sea creatures, are shown in a sort of X-ray skeletal form showing ribs and joints with oval shaped eyes and dismembered body parts used as 'fill-ins.'

The conical twined spruce root hat worn by the man on the left of the photograph was utilitarian, as well as being one of the most prestigious of crest objects. The flaring brim was typical of northern hats and the dress hat shown is of the chief's type which was worn to show off crest paintings. On the top are basketry cylinders in a stack. These stacks, which also appear carved on grave markers and totem poles, are often said to represent the number of potlatches given by the owner, although there is in fact no proof that this is so. The taller the stack the more prestige acquired by the wearer.

The man on the right is wearing a metal nose ring and has a facial painting or tattoo. In his right hand he holds a wooden rattle of intricate design. The men are standing in front of one of the wooden houses built from large cedar wood planks and which were used for dances and ceremonies as well as store houses for all manner of goods and sleeping quarters.

Tlingit

Coastal and Inland Tlingit. Na-Dene language family.

*T*his 1905 photograph by Edward M. Kindle shows young children playing with a model boat and inside a small canoe in Taku Harbor, Alaska. They appear to show no fear of the water, as would be natural for a people whose existence depended on water. The Tlingit were famous for their skills as canoe builders, as well as carving, painting and the working of copper. Less creditable to them in the old days was their fame as slavers and they made long expeditions for the purpose of obtaining these.

The variety of Northwest Coast canoe types was immense, as can be imagined of a maritime people, but the largest was probably made by the Haida who had seven basic styles. Some of these large canoes were sixty feet (18m) long and could be used as war vehicles when paddled by several servants or slaves.

The Tlingit were especially fond of these Haida canoes and they were often bought by wealthy men for the purposes of war or trading expeditions. The Tlingit themselves also had a variety of canoes such as the small boats which women used for fishing and traveling short journeys. There were also special canoes for seal hunting which had polished bases to speed them through the water, and were usually kept on platforms to protect the bottoms.

The big canoes were often decorated with their owner's crests and special ones were given names. These had swept-up prows which extended over the front and which were often carved with figures of animals or mythological beings which looked a little like figureheads.

The manufacture of the large dugout canoes was a lengthy and skilled process mostly done with stone or bone adzes, mauls and wedges of the same material. When iron was available it made the job easier but many of the more elderly craftsmen still preferred the old tools.

The Subarctic

**AHTNA • ATTIKAMEK • BEAVER • CARRIER
CHILCOTIN • CHIPEWYAN • CREE
DOGRIB • HAN • HARE • HOLIKACHUK
INGALIK • KASKA • KOLCHAN • KOYUKON
KUTCHIN • MONTAGNAIS • NASKAPI • OJIBWA
SAULTEAUX • SEKANI • SLAVEY • TAHLTAN
TANANA • INLAND TLINGIT • TUTCHONE
YELLOWKNIFE**

*T*he vast inland area of northern North America from Alaska right across to the Labrador coast was the home of the Athabascan and Algonquian peoples. To the west their lives were almost entirely centered around the caribou, with some sea fishing, but in the east they lived a pastoral and hunting existence. At several points their cultures merged with those of other areas - the Arctic, the Northwest Coast, the Northeast and the Plains, for example. The western groups lived in a harsh environment and great cultural achievements were few. But with the coming of fur traders and the introduction of trade goods, which included beads, all these people developed a distinct style for the decoration of their clothing and equipment. In the east some crops were grown and wild rice and maple sugar were gathered, but in this land of forests, lakes and rivers, hunting and fishing were the main means of subsistence. The forests were full of animal life, and the birchbark canoe was developed for use on the lakes and rivers.
Naturally, the fur trade embroiled the tribes as strings of trading posts spread across the area and the seasonal gathering of furs became of paramount importance. Coming to rely almost entirely on trade goods the people were left vulnerable once the fur-bearing animals had been virtually trapped out.

A Montagnais and Naskapi camp photographed in 1883. The central interior of the provinces of Quebec and the Labrador Peninsula, above the St Lawrence River, is home to these nomadic hunters and fishermen. The two tribes are closely related.

Ahtna

Upper and Lower Ahtna. Athabascan language family.

Sometimes erroneously called Ahtena, this small group lived in the Copper River basin of southern Alaska and were known as great traders of native copper, animal skins and hides and, later, trade goods, which they obtained first from the Russians and then from the gold seekers and fur traders.

Hunting and fishing were the chief occupations of the men whilst the women processed the food and made all the clothing. Probably the most important food was the sockeye salmon, which was caught in the rivers with dip nets and traps as well as harpoons. Game such as caribou, dall sheep, mountain goats and moose were hunted with bows and arrows and killed in pitfall and deadfall traps. Birds such as wildfowl, ptarmigan and spruce grouse were eaten as well as small mammals, berries and vegetables.

The two girls in the photograph, taken in 1902, are the daughters of Chief Stickwan. They are using the 'tump line,' an essential piece of equipment in these regions for carrying loads, which are also supported by a strap across the chest. Often these were intricately decorated with porcupine quillwork or woven in native-dyed fibers. The word 'tump,' literally to 'carry a deer through the woods after it had been killed,' comes from the Algonquian word 'madumbi' meaning a pack or burden strap.

The girl on the left is wearing a cloth dress with convenient pocket and the other girl has a similar dress but made in the native style and decorated across the shoulders, sleeve ends and neck with pearl buttons, a popular trade item in this area. She is also wearing one-piece trouser moccasins which were worn by men and women and, amongst the wealthy, were decorated with quills and, later, beads. Both girls have the almost obligatory trade kettle for cooking and tea-making.

Koyukon

Upper, Lower and Koyukok River Koyukon. Athabascan language family.

Three sub-divisions of this tribe lived in the vast area of the central Alaskan plateau and were primarily hunters, with fishing as a secondary means of subsistence. Each division had a distinct culture of its own, dependent on its environment. Those of the Lower group and those living along the Koyokuk River had close associations with the Inupiat-Inuit, whose lifestyle they emulated. Their beliefs, social structure and aspects of their ceremonial life differed from that of the other division. Those of the Upper group had relations with, and traded with, the Tanana, their cousins from the southeast. The vast area of the country itself also had considerable variations from huge areas of forests, lowland flats with marshes and lakes and, in the northern areas, arid uplands and mountains. Little tribal unity was recognized and it was not until the arrival of whites that tribal chiefs were appointed to organize the people into more manageable groups.

The Russians were the first to make contact in 1838 but the 1890s saw the influx of gold prospectors and by 1898 the whole area was swarming with people who were then followed by the missionaries.

The photograph, taken in the early 1900s, shows a family dressed in winter clothing of caribou-skin parkas trimmed with fur, possibly wolverine. This and wolf skin was often used around the face because it was slower to freeze from the wearer's breath than other furs. The small girl on the right appears to be wearing a parka made from white hare skins. During the summer similar clothing would be worn but the skins would have been dehaired.

Saulteaux

Algonquian language family.

The Saulteaux occupied a territory around Lake Winnipeg in Manitoba that stretched back into Ontario. The southern limits were on the Canada-United States border.

Fish was a major source of food for them and, during the spring and early summer, there would be communal activity at the lakes and rivers where fish were caught in nets, or speared at fish weirs. They were then cleaned, dried and smoked. It was a time for the renewal of social ties and family reunions and a general 'get-together' for all the people. As winter approached, small bands would set out to continue some fishing but mostly to trap and hunt game. Moose, elk and caribou were taken in traps and with bows and arrows as well as spears. In later times the trapping of fur-bearing animals became a priority. When duck and geese returned in the early spring they were taken in nets or shot with bows and arrows over ingeniously-made decoys. Wild rice and maple syrup was also gathered.

The two apprehensive-looking men in the photograph, taken in a studio by J.F. Rowe in the 1890s, are identified as Charlie Assiniboine and his brother, Saulteaux, the sons of Assiniboine, a chief of the Portage band from southern Manitoba. They are wearing beautifully-beaded clothing of post-contact material as well as quite incongruous straw hats, in one of which appears to be a bunch of flowers!

Their blue trade-cloth leggings are decorated in a beautiful floral style of great skill and elegance and their moccasins are of the soft-sole, one-piece type with beaded insteps above the puckered toes. The man on the left has loom-beaded garters and holds a 'spontoon'-type tomahawk. He also has two very fine beaded bandolier bags across his shoulders, such decorative accessories, being expensive and requiring great skill to make, were worn as prestige items.

Tahltan

Athabascan language family.

This tribe were amongst a small group originally known as the Nahane and their territory was the drainage basin of the Stikine River in northwestern British Columbia. This land was mostly deciduous and coniferous forest with wide, open parkland, and the people were hunters and trappers eating mostly meat, with fish in times of necessity - although there was a plentiful supply of salmon to be had in the spring and summer. In winter the tribe would split into small bands to go hunting. Moose, caribou, wood buffalo, bear and mountain sheep and goats were the big game animals, and snowshoes were often used in the pursuit of them. Unlike their coastal neighbors they used canoes sparingly, and those they did were of poor quality. Before the advent of white traders, much trading was carried on with the Tlingit and other coastal tribes. The inland Tahltan exchanged hides, furs, sinew, snowshoes, copper and food commodities with the coastal people for wooden boxes and pipes, dentalium and other shells and eulachon (candlefish) oil, over what became knows as 'grease trails.'

The couple in the photograph, taken about 1906 by G.T. Emmons, are Koshon Old Wolf and his wife Thlogosquin. They are wearing a mixture of native costume and trade materials. Thlogosquin wears an animal-skin cloak over her cloth dress while he has on a tunic-type shirt with stylized beadwork very similar to Tlingit work, cloth trousers, skin moccasins and a high fur hat.

In the early days clothing would have been made from caribou or moose hide, but during the nineteenth century European clothing gradually replaced this, except for the boot-type leggings which remained in use to the end of the century for winter warmth. The Tahltan were reported as not being very artistic and much of their ceremonial clothing was bought from the Tlingit, probably in trade.

The Arctic

ALEUT • INUPIAT-INUIT • YUP'IK

The 'Land of the Midnight Sun', a land of ice and snow extending from the Aleutian Islands and the northeastern tip of Siberia in the west, through the coastal area of southern Alaska up and around the coast and across northernmost Canada and into Greenland in the east. The direct distance is more than 3,000 miles (4,800km) - perhaps as much as 6,000 miles (9,600km) if the undulating coastlines are accounted for.

It is inhabited by people originally from the Russian mainland, probably the last migration across the Bering Straits, a land inhospitable to the white man but home to the hunters and fishermen who have made their lives there. Although life is a continual battle against the elements the people tht live there have, over thousands of years, adapted to this environment and have become a part of the ecosystem.

Three main culture groups have evolved: the Aleut, the Yup'ik and the Inupiat-Inuit - formerly referred to as Eskimo. During the long winters they live snugly in semi-subterranean houses and hunt seals on the ice as well as walrus and occasionally whales. They also find fish through holes in the ice. In summertime they travel inland to harvest salmon from the rivers and hunt the caribou. For travel the people had sledges of many kinds, mostly pulled by teams of dogs. For river and sea travel the skin-covered kayak was ideal as a one-man means of transport. Today they have not been slow to take advantage of the white man's technology, but with such advantages have come disadvantages in the form of disease and pollution.

Mainland Southwest Alaska Eskimo of the Yup'ik family , photographed in about 1877 outside their storage houses at Togiak. The buildings look rather like log cabins and in fact are probably made of split timbers and have wooden doors. The roofs are sod-covered with dried vegetation or straw, which is held in place with netting. The people all appear to be wearing native clothing and one man is sporting a fur hat.

Inupiat-Inuit

Baffinland Eskimo, Bering Strait Eskimo, Caribou Eskimo, Copper Eskimo, West Greenland Eskimo, Iglulik, Interior North Alaska Eskimo, Inuit of Quebec, Inupiat, Kotzebue Sound Eskimo, Labrador Coast Eskimo, Mackenzie Delta Eskimo, Netsilik, Polar Eskimo, St. Lawrence Island Eskimo and Siberian Eskimo. Inupiaq language family.

These children from St. Lawrence Island were photographed in 1888. They are all wearing caribou-skin parkas with the hair-side in. Fashion decreed that the boys follow the men in having the top of the head shaved whilst the girls and women kept their hair long and loose, or in braids. These people occupy an island off the coast of Siberia, which is probably the last remaining piece of the last Ice Age land bridge which joined Siberia and Alaska some 30,000 years ago. They are culturally more closely related, through language and many of their customs, to the Asiatic Eskimo population of Siberia than those of North America.

Quite early on they were involved with the commercial whaling activities of the Russians and Americans, and although they had the advantages of obtaining firearms and other goods, they also received diseases and the usual lowering of moral standards brought about by the influx of these people. They suffered a catastrophic famine in the winter of 1878-79 caused, so the story goes, by the people being given large amounts of liquor by the whalers at a time when they should have been on the annual walrus hunt for their winter food stocks. This was followed by a spell of harsh weather so bad that even those who wanted to hunt were unable to do so. Starvation and sickness followed, ending in the deaths of some 1,500 people; a tragedy from which they never really recovered. Their survivors today still make most of their living from the sea by hunting whales, walrus and seals as well as an occasional polar bear.

Inupiat-Inuit

Baffinland Eskimo, Bering Strait Eskimo, Caribou Eskimo, Copper Eskimo, West Greenland Eskimo, Iglulik, Interior North Alaska Eskimo, Inuit of Quebec, Inupiat, Kotzebue Sound Eskimo, Labrador Coast Eskimo, Mackenzie Delta Eskimo, Netsilik, Polar Eskimo, St. Lawrence Island Eskimo and Siberian Eskimo. Inupiaq language family.

*U*nfortunately there is no record of where this man comes from or to which group he belongs. He is wearing a gut or intestine parka and skin trousers. Such garments were made by the women who processed the skins and did all the sewing - both men and women wore similar clothing.

Among the Aleuts such gut parkas were made from horizontal strips of walrus intestine sewn together and decorated with feathers, down and colored yarns. The Yup'ik of southwest Alaska wore their gut parkas with the arms through slits in the sides, more convenient when working than using the almost nonfunctional sleeves. Parkas were also originally made of bird skins, and later of caribou skin, and worn with the hair-side in. The St Lawrence Island people wore gutskin parkas over their other clothing for protection. These were made of seal and walrus gut that was soaked, scraped clean and then inflated to dry. Its opaque texture was obtained by exposure to the sun. The use of gut parkas seems to have declined amongst the Canadian Eskimo who used an incredible variety of materials for their clothing. The families of good hunters replacing their clothing every year, whilst poorer people made theirs last for more than a year and used sealskin which was more easily obtainable than caribou. These people also used eider duck skins mixed with seal and dog skin in their parkas. Polar bear skins were used for men's pants and boots, while fox, fish and hare skins were for women and children. Fawn and unborn caribou skins were used for infants. Caribou skin clothing reached its height in the Subarctic area with the production of coats of this skin by the Naskapi Indians.

Inupiat-Inuit

Baffinland Eskimo, Bering Strait Eskimo, Caribou Eskimo, Copper Eskimo, West Greenland Eskimo, Iglulik, Interior North Alaska Eskimo, Inuit of Quebec, Inupiat, Kotzebue Sound Eskimo, Labrador Coast Eskimo, Mackenzie Delta Eskimo, Netsilik, Polar Eskimo, St. Lawrence Island Eskimo and Siberian Eskimo. Inupiaq language family.

These Polar Eskimo are the northernmost human population in the world and are located mostly on the northwest coast of Greenland with another group on the east coast.

These two girls - Arnaruniak (left) and Inalliak (right) - were photographed by Thomas N. Krabbe in 1909. They are both wearing costumes of skin consisting of coats and long thigh-length boots. The girl on the left also has a hood and is wearing skin mittens. The skins used for these garments were probably dehaired sealskin which was dried in the very cold weather in order to give it stiffness. Under their long boots women wore a form of stockings made of caribou or hare skin: the upper part of these stockings was loose enough to be used for carrying or storing small objects. Short trousers of fox skin were also used and, under these, small underpants of seal skin were worn. Under their seal-skin outer coats women wore another coat of either seal or fox skin in the winter. For carrying a baby other coats of seal or fox skin with extra large hoods, in which the baby could be put, were used. Various methods of skin preparation were used depending on the animal and the use for which the skin was needed. Seal skins were scraped clean and then stretched and dried. If it was necessary to remove any remaining fat they were then soaked in urine or, in later times, detergents, following which they were again dried, scraped and rubbed to soften them. Animal sinew, particularly that from the back of the caribou, was used for sewing.

Inupiat-Inuit

Baffinland Eskimo, Bering Strait Eskimo, Caribou Eskimo, Copper Eskimo, West Greenland Eskimo, Iglulik, Interior North Alaska Eskimo, Inuit of Quebec, Inupiat, Kotzebue Sound Eskimo, Labrador Coast Eskimo, Mackenzie Delta Eskimo, Netsilik, Polar Eskimo, St. Lawrence Island Eskimo and Siberian Eskimo. Inupiaq language family.

*L*ike most Eskimo the people of Alaska lived by hunting and land animals such as caribou, bear, musk ox and many small rodents played an important part in their subsistence, as well as the harvest from the sea in the form of the many varieties of seals, whales and walrus. They lived in houses made from wood and sod, which were semi-subterranean and contained one or more closely related families. There was often also a man's house, which acted as a social center for the men, as well as a dance house. Women were also entitled to some use of this place. Most Eskimo decorated themselves to some degree, face and body tattooing being a common practice for both men and women. A girl at puberty had a tattoo line from the edge of her lower lip to the chin and when she was married further lines were added. Amongst men - such as these North Alaska Eskimo photographed in 1880 - tattooing was sometimes a mark of distinction and a great whale hunter might prick the number of his catches on his arms, cheeks or chest. Other designs were merely for decorative purposes.

The other distinctive form of decoration, the labret, may be seen in the picture. These men have punctured a hole below each corner of the mouth and inserted two of these objects, which were generally made of bone, ivory, shell or wood. Men's lips were pierced at puberty and the holes gradually enlarged by the use of increasingly large plugs until the final button-shaped plugs were inserted. The different sized plugs were often kept after use as a souvenir. Some of the men in the picture also have hair bands of beads or strips of copper.

THE ARCTIC
Inupiat-Inuit

Baffinland Eskimo, Bering Strait Eskimo, Caribou Eskimo, Copper Eskimo, West Greenland Eskimo, Iglulik, Interior North Alaska Eskimo, Inuit of Quebec, Inupiat, Kotzebue Sound Eskimo, Labrador Coast Eskimo, Mackenzie Delta Eskimo, Netsilik, Polar Eskimo, St. Lawrence Island Eskimo and Siberian Eskimo. Inupiaq language family.

*T*he westernmost group, these Copper Eskimo occupied the areas of Victoria Island and onto the Canadian Mainland known as the Northwest Territories, down to the district of Mackenzie with Bear Island in the southwestern corner and the Victoria Straits in the east.

Hunting and fishing were their means of livelihood and both activities varied according to the area and the migration patterns of caribou and fish. Fishing from weirs was practiced during August when the Arctic char returned to the inland waters to breed, as did the salmon in the spring. In other areas, because of the huge herds, hunting caribou was of more importance than fishing. Geese and ducks, as well as the occasional musk ox, supplemented the diet in the summer and there was usually a lull in hunting for a few weeks in November before the hunting of seals through holes in the ice began. Occasional forays after polar bears were also another winter activity.

The photograph by Diamond Jenness shows Copper Eskimo people using a series of stone weirs or dams to catch salmon. Men, women and children took part in this method of impaling the fish with spears and tridents. The practice of spearing fish by torchlight, as carried out by their Indian neighbors, was impractical to these people as, apart from the lack of bark from which to make torches, there was, of course, no darkness during the summer time when the waters were free of ice. Materials such as brush for baskets and fish traps were also unavailable so the people used the only available material, ie stone, for their fish traps.

The Northeast

**ABENAKI • ALGONQUIAN • CAYUGA
CHICKAHOMINY • CHIPPEWA (OJIBWA)
DELAWARE • FOX • HURON • ILLINOIS
IROQUOIS • KICKAPOO • MAHICAN • MALISEET-
PASSAMAQUODDY • MATTAPONY
MENOMINEE • MIAMI • MICMAC • MOHAWK
NANTICOKE • NIPISSING • ONEIDA
ONONDAGA • OTTAWA • PEQUOT
POTAWATOMI • POWHATAN • SAUK • SENECA
SHAWNEE • SUSQUEHANNOCK • TUSCARORA
WAMPANOAG • WINNEBAGO**

*T*aking in the Great Lakes and surrounding countryside, the Northeast and its woodlands extended eastwards, south of the St Lawrence River to the Atlantic coast and the present-day Canadian provinces of New Brunswick and Nova Scotia, then southwards down to Virginia and parts of North Carolina.
A grand mixture of languages and cultures covered this area, but around the Great Lakes and southwards the dominant tribes were those of the Iroquois, a confederacy of five tribes (six after 1726) who were prominent in the colonial wars between the English, French and Dutch. The Europeans traded on the Indian's traditions of inter-tribal fighting and, arming their favorites, set them against one another in bloody warfare lasting more than a century. In the north the less powerful Chippewa lived in scattered bands farming, hunting and fishing, using their elegant birchbark canoes. Eastwards, the people were the first to be contacted by the white newcomers and many small tribes were lost in the wars of colonization; others became Europeanized and soon lost their identities; most of those remaining then lost their land as the new nation expanded its territory at their expense.

Sauk chief Pa-She-Pa-Ho and a council of his tribe in 1885. These people have now become known as the Sauk and Fox but had been quite distinct entities since early times , although closely linked, and lived southwest of Lake Michigan.

SAUK AND FOX
CHIEF AND COUNCIL

Chippewa

Chippewa (Ojibwa). Algonquian language family.

A photograph of Chippewa dancers at a Fourth of July celebration on the Red Lake Reservation in Minnesota in about 1908. Most of the men have had their hair cut short and have lost their braids. The structure is called a 'dance arbor' and is usually in circular form, the drum and drummers seated in the center with the dancers stepping around them. Green boughs and branches would be thrown over the top for coolness. In spite of persecution by the whites, the Fourth of July was usually a good excuse for a dance and a Pow Wow when families and friends could get together and recreate some of the old customs. Such Pow Wows are still important today in bringing old and new friends together to help form bonds as in the old days. Today they are also a means for the younger elements of the tribes to earn large prize money in competitions for costume and dancing, for which there are many categories. At the larger Pow Wows Indians will come together from all over the United States and Canada to compete and socialize. Known as the 'Pow Wow circuit,' many families will spend the whole summer traveling from one to another, and often a great part of the winter making special dance costumes for sons and daughters or grandchildren to show off in during the summer season. In the old days dances were held for a variety of reasons, the most obvious of which was the War Dance to engender a spirit of belligerence in warriors departing on the warpath. Dances were also held as victory celebrations if such war parties had returned successfully. Warrior and religious societies also had dances for special occasions, some continuing for many days interspersed with various ceremonies.

WACOMO.   SAC & FO. 21.

Fox

Algonquian language family.

The Mesquakie or Red Earth people, commonly called the Fox and closely associated with the Sauk, lived originally to the west of Lake Michigan on the Wisconsin River but moved gradually southward, ending up in Iowa along the banks of the Mississippi. They were a restless and aggressive people who were constantly at war with their neighbors and the French whom they hated for arming their enemies against them. Together with the Sauk they drove the Illinois out and occupied their land. They occasionally allied themselves with the Sioux and the Iroquois but were finally defeated by the combined Chippewa, Menominee and Potawatomi who were organized by the French against them.

When not fighting, the Fox were horticulturists hunting in the winter months and living in bark-covered houses in the summer or in wigwam-type dwellings of small parties on the winter hunt. They also hunted buffalo, much like the Plains Indians, but this source of food finished about 1820 when these animals were no longer to be seen in their hunting territory.

The fearsome warrior in the photograph taken in 1868 is Wah-Com-Mo or Fast Walker. He wears a traditional Prairie Indian outfit. He has a striped trade shirt and wool trade blanket with cloth leggings and beaded moccasins. He has a deer hair roach over his own roached hairstyle, from which hangs an eagle feather, and he is carrying an eagle feather fan and a spontoon-type tomahawk, which appears more decorative than lethal.

The pride of his outfit is the fine necklace of grizzly bear claws - rare and very valuable . To obtain these trophies set a man aside as one of great valor and he wore them with pride. There were many construction styles for these objects and the one worn by Fast Walker is a particularly fine one, the base being wrapped with otter skin, the tail of which probably hangs down his back.

Seneca

Iroquoian language family.

The Seneca were one of the largest of the five nations of the Iroquois Confederacy and inhabited western New York state from Seneca Lake to Lake Erie. They were influential and prominent in carrying out the Iroquois policy of conquering lesser tribes who were then drawn into the confederacy. They were much involved in the bloody wars which raged in and around this area, sometimes siding with the French but generally on better terms with the British. They espoused the British cause during the American Revolution but suffered for their efforts in the long term when, with the defeat of the British, they were dispersed and lost most of their lands. The haunting studio portrait of the pensive Carolyn G. Parker, or Hanging Flower, is almost identical to another which shows her standing, wearing exactly the same costume, and is a copy of an apparently lost daguerreotype which had been hand tinted and the image reversed when printed. Both were taken in about 1895 and show her in traditional costume beautifully decorated by herself with beadwork, brooches and silver ornaments.

Ely S. Parker, her brother, who was of Seneca and Huron descent, acquired an academic education and at the outbreak of the Civil War was employed as an engineer at the home of Ulysses S. Grant with whom he became friendly. He joined the Union Army and due to his outstanding service was made assistant adjutant-general with the rank of Captain. He worked as secretary to General Grant and, because of their friendship and the fact of Parker's beautiful handwriting, was able to handle all the general's personal and official affairs. Following a brilliant career in the army he retired in 1869 and was made Commissioner of Indian Affairs by President Grant. Retiring in 1871 he took many other government posts as well as being a valuable informant to the anthropologist Lewis Henry Morgan. He died in 1895, the year his sister's picture was taken.

Winnebago

Siouan language family.

The Winnebago, who had been moved to Nebraska in the 1800s, still kept their horticultural traditions but enthusiasm for gardening on the small lots given them gradually waned with the general discontent and injustice of their removal and they began to lease their farms to whites and the consequent profits accumulated so that they became moderately rich. However, after a degree of prosperity the money was soon dissipated on the tempting goods of the white man and they became easy targets for unscrupulous whites and demoralization set in. Those who stayed or returned to Wisconsin were eventually allocated scattered homesteads on the poorest land and somehow survived with a few of their old customs intact.

During these troubled times it was with difficulty that family life was able to flourish but, like all Indian mothers, they treated their children with much love and care as an important part of the tribal entity. In most tribes women were highly respected members of the community and had their own sphere of responsibility and duties which they learnt in the course of their upbringing. They had many tasks to perform as well as raising children and their contribution was well recognized by the opposite sex. The photograph of this refined looking woman, Nellie Kingsley, and her son, Andrew Blackhawk, was taken in 1913 by C.J. Van Schaick in the Black River Falls area of Wisconsin.

Winnebago

Siouan language family.

*T*his picture shows Black Hawk and Winneshiek of the Winebago. The tribe occupied the land around Green Bay in what is now Wisconsin and were surrounded by the Sac and Fox to the south and the Menominee in the north. They were a sedentary horticultural people hunting game in the winter.

They were continually harassed by neighboring tribes and through contact with the first Europeans suffered two smallpox outbreaks before 1836 which wiped out more than one-quarter of the tribe. They were moved and resettled many times but remained loyal to the French until their power in Canada waned when they sided with the British. They were prominent in the war of 1812 and fought together with the Sac and Fox in the Black Hawk War. Some small groups remain in Wisconsin but the rest were moved to a reservation in Nebraska in 1874 where their remnants live today.

The two men, photographed sometime before 1900, were important leaders in resisting removal from their homelands. Black Hawk has on a white man's coat while his comrade wears a white shirt, beaded apron and possibly leggings with beaded garters. They are both wearing the distinctive but traditional otter-fur turbans which were made in many varieties and had quite a wide distribution. The one worn by Black Hawk uses the head and body of the otter but not the tail, the decoration appears to be of beadwork, sometimes ribbon appliqué was used, with a feather tassel hanging from the otter's head. The other one is of a similar style and is also decorated with stylized floral beadwork and beaded rosettes or medallions. The use of otter fur for these singular headdresses has old connections to the Medicine Dance Society because the otter was associated with the original myths and rites of this society.

Bibliography

The Southeast

Anon. 'Seminole Patchwork' in *American Indian Hobbyist Magazine*, Vol VI, No 1/2.

Debo, A. *The Rise and Fall of the Choctaw Republic*. University of Oklahoma Press, Norman. 1961.

Feder. N. 'Otter Fur Turbans' in *American Indian Tradition Magazine*, Vol 7, No 3.

Howard, J.H. & Levine, V.L. *Choctaw Music and Dance*. University of Oklahoma Press, Norman. 1990.

Howard, J.H. *Oklahoma Seminole Medicines, Magic and Religion*. University of Oklahoma Press, Norman. 1984.

Johnson, M.G. 'Surviving Southeast Groups' in *American Indian Craft and Culture Magazine*, Vol 5, No 10.

Lanford, B. 'Winnebago Bandoleer Bags' in *American Indian Art Magazine*, Summer 1984, Vol 9, No 3.

Wood, G. 'Seminole Moccasins' in *American Indian Crafts and Culture Magazine*, Vol 5, No 3.

The Southwest

Broder, P.J. *Taos, A Painter's Dream*. New York Graphic Society, Little Brown & Co, New York. 1980.

Dutton, B. *Navaho and Apache: The Athabascan Peoples*. Prentice-Hall, New Jersey. 1975.

James, H.C. *Pages from Hopi History*. University of Arizona Press, Tucson. 1974.

Russell, F. *The Pima Indians*. University of Arizona Press, Tucson 1975.

Tanner, C.L. 'The Naja' in *American Indian Art Magazine*, Spring 1982, Vol 7, No 2.

Witherspoon, G. 'Navaho Social Organization' in *Handbook of North American Indians*, Smithsonian Institute, Washington, 1978, Vol 10.

The Plains

Bancroft-Hunt, N. & Forman, W. *The Indians of the Great Plains*. Orbis Publishing, London.,1985.

Dunraven, Earl of. *The Great Divide*. Chatto and Windus, London. 1876.

Ewers, J.C. *Indian Life on the Upper Missouri*. University of Oklahoma Press, Norman. 1988.

Feder, N. 'Pawnee Cradle Boards' in *American Indian Art Magazine*, Autumn 1978, Vol 3, No 4.

Grinnell, G.B. *The Cheyenne Indians*. 2 Vols. Yale University Press, Newhaven. 1923.

Kroeber, A.L. *The Arapaho*. University of Nebraska Press, Lincoln. 1983.

La Flesche, F. & Fletcher, A.C. *The Omaha Tribe*. 2 Vols. University of Nebraska Press, Lincoln. 1972.

Nye, W.S. *Plains Indian Raiders*. University of Oklahoma Press, Norman. 1968.

Seton, E.T. *The Book of Woodcraft and Indian Lore*. Constable & Co, London. 1912.

Stegner, W. *Wolf Willow*. University of Nebraska Press, Lincoln. 1980.

Vestal, S. *Sitting Bull: Champion of the Sioux*. University of Oklahoma Press, Norman. 1956.

Wallace, E. & Adamson Hoebel, E. *The Comanche: Lords of the South Plains*. University of Oklahoma Press, Norman. 1952.

Webb, W.P. *The Great Plains*. Grosset & Dunlap, New York. 1931.

Wissler, C. 'Societies and Dance Associations of the Blackfoot Indians' in

Anthropological Papers, American Museum of Natural History Vol XI, Part IV, New York. 1913.

Plateau and Basin

Haines, F. *Indians of the Great Basin and Plateau*. Putnam's Sons, New York. 1970.

Haines, F. *The Nez Perce: Tribesmen of the Columbia Plateau*. University of Oklahoma Press, Norman. 1955.

Madsen, B.D. *The Northern Shoshone*. Caxton Printers, Caldwell, Idaho. 1980.

McWhorter, L.V. *Yellow Wolf: His Own Story*. Caxton Printers, Caldwell, Idaho. 1948.

Murphy, R.F. & Y. 'Northern Shoshone and Bannock' in *Handbook of North American Indians*, Smithsonian Institute, Washington, 1978, Vol II.

Pettit, J. *Utes, The Mountain People*. Johnson Books, Boulder Colorado. 1990.

California

Bates, C.D. & Bibby, B. 'Flicker Quill Bands of the Maidu' in *American Indian Art Magazine*, Autumn 1980, Vol 5, No 4.

Bates, C.D. 'Feather Belts of Central California' in *American Indian Art Magazine*, Winter 1981, Vol 7, No 1.

Bean, L.J. & Theodoratus, D. 'Western Pomo and Northeastern Pomo' in *Handbook of North American Indians*, Smithsonian Institute, Washington, 1978, Vol 7.

Bean, L.J. & BrakkeVan, S. 'Cults and their Transformation' in *Handbook* (op. cit), Vol 8.

Gould, R.A. 'Tolowa' in *Handbook* (op cit), Vol 8.

James, G.W. *Indian Basketry*. Dover Publications, New York. 1972.

Museum, Bowers, Santa Anna, California. *Indian Basketry*. Brook House, Los Angeles, California. 1977.

Pilling, A.R. 'Yorok' in *Handbook* (op cit), Vol 8.

The Northwest Coast

Blackman, M.B. 'Haida: Tradition and Culture' in *Handbook of North American Indians*, Smithsonian Institute, Washington, 1978, Vol 7.

Codere, H. 'Kwakiult: Tradition and Culture' in *Handbook* (op cit), Vol 7.

De Laguna, F. 'Tlingit' in *Handbook* (op cit), Vol 7.

Hawthorne, A. *Kwakiutl Art*. University of Washington Press, Seattle. 1978.

Holm, W. 'Art' in *Handbook* (op cit), Vol 7.

Holm, W. *Crooked Beak of Heaven*. Thomas Burke Memorial, University of Washington Press, Seattle. 1974.

Rohner, R.P. & E.C. *The Kwakiutl Indians of British Columbia*. Holt, Rhinehart and Winston, University of Connecticut. 1970.

Ruby, H.R. & Brown, J.A. *Myron Eells and the Puget Sound Indians*. Superior Publishing Co, Seattle, Washington. 1976.

Suttles, W. 'Environment' in *Handbook* (op cit), Vol 7.

The Subarctic

Athaspaskans: Strangers of the North. The National Museum of Man, Ottawa, Canada. 1974.

Burnham, D.K. *To Please the Caribou*. Royal Ontario Museum, Toronto, Canada. 1992.